Vladimir Soloviev

EMPIRE
OF CORRUPTION

The territory of the Russian national pastime

Glagoslav Publications

EMPIRE OF CORRUPTION

The territory of the Russian national pastime

by Vladimir Soloviev

First published in Russian as "Империя коррупции.
Территория русской национальной игры"

Translated from the Russian by Matthew Hyde

© 2012, Vladimir Soloviev

© 2014, Glagoslav Publications, United Kingdom

Glagoslav Publications Ltd
88-90 Hatton Garden
EC1N 8PN London
United Kingdom

www.glagoslav.com

ISBN: 978-1-78267-071-1

A catalogue record for this book is available
from the British Library.

CONTENTS

FOREWORD 6

CHAPTER 1 8

CHAPTER 2 19

CHAPTER 3 31

CHAPTER 4 39

CHAPTER 5 50

CHAPTER 6 62

CHAPTER 7 84

CHAPTER 8 91

CHAPTER 9 99

CHAPTER 10 120

CHAPTER 11 135

CHAPTER 12 144

CHAPTER 13 151

AFTERWORD 172

Corruption — spoiling, putrefaction, collapse, decay, decline, depravity, perversion.

Anglo-Russian Dictionary
of General Vocabulary

FOREWORD

The fight against corruption is Russia's national sport. Everyone is fighting corruption. But judging by the fact that every new leader identifies this as one of his main goals, corruption inevitably wins. Why? Is it some sort of awful ailment, which, despite all our efforts, it is impossible to cure. Or maybe we are trying to fight something which is not, in the broadly accepted sense, corruption at all, but something altogether different. Meaning that all our efforts are always doomed to failure.

As soon as Dmitry Medvedev became president, he set up two Commissions. The first was aimed at improving the operation of the justice system, the second was tasked with the fight against corruption. All of the leading experts were summoned. Several years passed, and, as I understand it, the fight against corruption still remains one of the main goals of the government — even if a lot has been achieved in the field. Government officials have been obliged to complete income declarations which are then publically discussed, a number of generals were dismissed for providing inaccurate information in their declarations, and one of them was even subject to legal proceedings. However, there was no breakthrough in the public consciousness.

I have to say that when I hear discussions about corruption, they always seem to be closer to literature, rather than the law. People quote Karamzin, who wrote that theft was commonplace in Russia, and always will be. They recall Saltykov-Shchedrin with a gesture of resignation and a sad smile, and continue to

6

thieve. One can't help being skeptical when one hears the latest summons to fight corruption, it's a bit like hearing that the bees have started to fight against honey. In the last few years at least work in the government structures has become desirable because of the high income — and of course that income is unofficial. Would this be possible without corruption? That's a rhetorical question of course. Asides from everything else, Russia's rating as a country to do business with is offensively low, and Russia maintains a stubbornly high position in the lists of countries which are dominated by corruption.

Everyone talks about corruption. But there are several fundamental misunderstandings at work. The main one is that when a policeman, or a traffic policeman, or a doctor, or a teacher, or a journalist take bribes, then they are all corrupt. But then what we see at the next level up we don't perceive as corruption — heaven forbid! — but administrative rent-seeking. It seems that we see those people sitting in the higher positions not as thieves, bribe-takers or criminals, but rentiers, who are just making the most out of their positions. From time to time, the public bridles, clutches its head and cries that this is too much, it can't go on, and then some sort of reaction against corruption begins. The government opens its eyes, turns its attention to the activities of Moscow city government under Mayor Luzhkov, recoils in shock and, after performing a series of complex ritual dances, dismisses Luzhkov. A number of Moscow district heads end up either in prison or under investigation. But, unfortunately, the larger system stays the same.

In this book we will certainly try to provide concrete examples of corruption, and descriptions of the corruption which pervades various state corporations, local government institutions, ministries and government departments. But most importantly, we will try to understand the woe which has befallen our country, and why we can't seem to be rid of it.

CHAPTER 1

Let's imagine for a moment that there is no corruption in the country. None at all. You go to the hospital for treatment, and it is completely free of corruption. So the nurses don't tidy up after the patients — you're welcome to clean the floors, take out the bedpans or change the sheets yourself if you want. And there is no medicine either. The next state allocation is due in three months — bad luck if the patient dies before then. An ambulance comes to pick up the elderly man, but the ambulance service isn't corrupt, so it leaves him where he is. Or it takes him to the closest hospital — so what if that one is no good, at least it's not corrupt.

The traffic police stop you, and they're also free from corruption. Which means that they have plenty of time on their hands. Plenty of time to carry out checks on you. You're pretty sure you haven't broken any laws, but they carry out check after check — all without any sign of corruption. The inspector has the right to check you, after all. Who knows, you might look suspicious, or a car the same colour and make as yours may have been reported stolen. The policeman has the whole working day ahead of him, it's no bother to him. You're the one with things to do, in a hurry to get somewhere. Maybe he suspects you've been drinking. Just a hunch, he could be mistaken, but it's only going to be proven for sure at the clinic - so off you go and give a sample. What do you mean you don't have the time? Surely you have a couple of hours set aside for just this kind of eventuality? We're very sorry, they say, but we're not corrupt, so please go calmly on your way.

It's wonderful that there is no corruption in the country. So your son or daughter can't get into university? They did well at school, but they're not from the region where everyone got 100% in their secondary school exams just for having pretty eyes, and they're not disabled. How are you going to explain that to them? 'Look, dear, life's just not fair'? Maybe.

Or you need some sort of document, like a certificate or statement. So you have to pass through the seven circles of hell to get it, and there are queues everywhere — all corruption-free. So everything takes so agonisingly long. Of course, you can make a fuss, and the newspapers will write about it. Of course, in our system anyone can be arrested and sent to prison. But what next?

Just don't try and tell me that all the officials, nurses, doctors and traffic police should be honest. They *are* honest -they don't take your money. But faced with your indignation, they will ask whether you would be prepared to come and work on their salaries — which, it turns out, are pretty small. Of course, you could ask them why they agreed to work for so little money in the first place. And it would be a perfectly reasonable question — just that there is no answer. Just like there is no one to help you. And no one will give you the document you need. And the nurse doesn't clean the hospital floors. But then you wouldn't go and work in her place.

By now we have begun to bitterly regret that the country is free of corruption, and we proclaim in unison: 'No, at that level it's not corruption, just the fair redistribution of money. It's clear that the state pays these people unfairly, so we just top up their salaries to make them commensurate with the work done.'

That could be right. But how much is fair? When we begin to investigate we discover to our surprise that we are still living in a socialist system, where a qualification-based pay scale remains in force. We explore further and realise with horror that it is impossible to live on the salaries paid under that pay scale. It turns out that there is simply not enough money in the country to pay everyone fairly. The pay scale works in such a way that if we try to raise the salary of a nurse in a regional hospital, we automatically increase all the salaries, right up to the Health Minister himself. So the disparity is not reduced, and the nurse's standard of living does not improve one bit. Of course we can always print more money, although doing so reduces the value of the money in circulation. But then at least everything will be fair, we say.

But what kind of fairness is it when good nurses and good doctors get the same salary as bad ones, we cry? As strange as it may seem, the bribes normally go to the best doctors and teachers, and the best health and education establishments. No one wants to pay money to end up in a bad hospital or send their children to a bad school. Indeed it seems very likely that without this money oiling the machine and, in effect, rewarding the best service providers, the country would be paralysed. I'm not thinking of the traffic police here. But then imagine how awful it would be if you were stopped for committing a minor traffic offence, and the police refused to take any money. Your punishment consists not only of the fine, but also of the time it takes to drive to the bank and stand in a queue. And the time you spend waiting for the penalty to be issued. What a hassle.

But that is just at the most basic, grassroots level. We encounter these practices every day, and no one is making much money out of them. But the next level up really annoys us. Here there is a common, naive, tendency to confuse corruption and extortion. Let's take, for example, unjustified tax inspections, or the use of criminal proceedings against a businessman to try to get money out of him. This is extortion rather than corruption, of course. The public thinks it is corruption, because law enforcement officials are taking the money, but it is a phenomenon of a different order. If we consider actual wage levels, and the way that money is really distributed within the system, we come to the unwelcome conclusion that many law enforcement agencies and security structures could easily use the designation PLC, as public limited companies, or worse still, OCG, as organised criminal gangs.

I always ask my audience, readers, and everyone who comes to my concerts one and the same question — do they think that if we all left the country there would be any corruption left behind? They chuckle and answer that of course not, if they all left, there would be no corruption left in Russia either. So then I ask them where the corruption comes from?

In reply they normally insist that the state is to blame for everything. It's generally believed that the ordinary citizen is blameless, that the state is always guilty. But then I ask them whether, if we all leave, the state stays behind? And suddenly it becomes clear that if we all up roots and leave, then there will be no state left either. What's more, when us Russians go and live in other countries, as a rule we become law-abiding citizens. Even if in the beginning we make efforts to corrupt the new system where we live, we quickly come to understand that these efforts are futile, coming up against the incorruptibility of the local law-enforcement officials, and we either see our days out in prison or come to our senses and live our lives as peaceful law-abiding citizens.

In order to understand the problem which is destroying us, we have to be quite clear that it is not five, nor ten, nor 15 years old. If we don't understand the history, we will never be free of corruption. For that very reason revelatory articles in newspapers, government edicts and public firing squads will change nothing. The next official will be appointed to the vacant position, and he will be exactly the same as the one before him. It is no surprise therefore that our analysts like to refer to the historical experience, raising a sad gaze to the ceiling and sighing that the theft of public money has always been common in Russia.

Let me quote document number PR342 P9A, published under the classification 'Top Secret' on 1 September 1922, and signed by the Deputy Chairman of the Council for Labor and

Defense, Rykov, and Deputy Secretary of the Council for Labor and Defense, Glyasser.

'The measures taken in the fight against bribe-taking and similar criminal offences can be described as following: Firstly, repressive-judicial measures increasing the legal sanctions for bribery and related crimes, swift court processes and hearing of cases, strengthening the apparatus of the investigatory organs for the fight against bribe-taking.

Secondly, legislative measures increasing the number of criminally punishable offences for different types of bribery, legislative regulation of the procedure, conditions and form of use of state organs for private mediation, and the introduction of public oversight over them.

Thirdly, legislative regulation of the statute and regulations on public service, joint ventures, intermediary activities and participation in private enterprises.

Fourthly, the cancelling of the system for issuing mandates and the legal regulation of the issuing of identity documents.

Measures for inspection and auditing: firstly — organizing at every stage oversight over contracts and subcontracting, and ensuring that subcontractors and contractors are honest in their commercial activities. Secondly — clarifying the question of conducting a precise audit of the number of sub-contractors and intermediaries within government departments, and between government departments. Thirdly, joint surprise checks and audits of criminal investigation organs.

Administrative measures — instructing all of the biggest economic organizations to compile a list of special persons with responsibility for the fight against corruption, and instructing that all complaints relating to corruption be dealt with to the shortest possible deadlines.

And fifthly, general measures — investigation and purging of all economic organizations at the central and local levels, with the aim of combating embezzlement and bribe-taking.'

Just think — ninety years have passed. And the sad but unavoidable conclusion is that absolutely nothing has changed, since bribery and embezzlement of public funds continue to flourish.

But let me pose the question: why has such thieving always taken place in Russia? And how did the word 'theft' begin to be used in this context? After all, theft is only possible when something doesn't belong to you. You can't thieve from yourself. Whenever we say that someone is thieving, we mean that they are taking someone else's property. But whose property exactly?

Of course we are unlikely to use the word corruption to describe a public servant who robs money and valuables from a neighbor's apartment under the cover of night. In this case he is a common thief, and of no interest to us, we are not dealing with him here. But who exactly is a public servant stealing from, if we describe him as corrupt? From the people? When Karamzin and Saltykov-Shchedrin were writing, it's unlikely anyone was particularly worried about the public good, but in the public consciousness a corrupt official was the same as a thief. And the victim of the theft was *de facto* the Tsar. Everything belonged to his Majesty the Emperor. No wonder that Nikolai II humbly referred to himself as 'Master of all the Lands of Russia' in the population census. It was the Tsar who was being robbed.

A public servant with his hand in the public purse was not taking what belonged to him, but what belonged to the Tsar. What is more, if he took Russian reality into account, he had to realize that although he may now be dressed in silk, the next day he could lose everything he had. After all, everything which he possessed had been gifted to him, and gifted only on a temporary basis — how long for exactly, only God knew. Historical experience showed that anyone who fell into disfavor could be deprived of their noble title, dismissed from work, and crushed to dust. Even if you were Menshikov himself, one day, sooner or later, your Berezovo would come. And you would see out your days not as a jolly retired courtier in your private palace somewhere in Nice or Cannes, but as a miserable sick old man in a wretched, earth-floored hut, lost in the boundless snow-planes, and every day you would look with horror into the eyes of your children, to whom you unable to leave anything behind. And this will depend not on whether you served the king honestly, but on whether his Highness the Emperor was feeling mischievous.

Even the concepts of honor or reputation therefore became highly conditional. Lermontov's description of the 'famous dishonesty of our honorable forefathers' is typical. Indeed, when we speak of ancient and distinguished families, the extent to which they really were ancient and distinguished is often highly exaggerated. The phrase from Alexandre Dumas' novels, 'he came from a noble but impoverished family' sounded out of place in the Russian context. We certainly understand the concept of impoverishment. But noble less so. Even the concept of noble families was rather vague. After all, our nobility used this term as a bad translation from the French and English. Who exactly were the nobility? The Orlovs? But can we really use the word nobility to describe the family of a man who shamed himself through regicide and as a result was ruthlessly humiliated by Tsar Paul, who forced Count Orlov to carry the crown during the re-burial of the remains of Peter III.

In fact there were very few of our nobles who could describe themselves and their ancestors with pride and respect, in the same way as their European colleagues could. It's hard for a person to speak of self-respect when you are being humiliated on an hourly basis by the Emperor, who owns you lock stock and barrel. It's just that a long time ago in England, or Spain, for example, something happened which never happened here in Russia. In England the king was forced to sign the Petition of Right, severely limiting the power of the monarch and defining the rights of the nobility. In Spain the Grandees would utter this ritual phrase during the coronation: 'We, who are no worse than you, are making you king, who is no better than us.'

The system which continued to exist in Russia was in essence a system of slavery, putting everyone from top to bottom into a position of subservience and dependence, a system in which your property and your life belonged to the Emperor. And as it transpired, in the grand scheme of things even robbing from him was not the greatest of sins — in any case sooner or later you would get the chop. And you didn't even need to thieve a snuff-box from someone's pocket, or a candelabrum off the table, you may have just been quietly putting a little bit aside for yourself.

The salary which you get from public service comes from the exchequer, which it is your job to fill. So in the grand scheme of things you are not actually thieving, you are just keeping a small percentage on commission for yourself. The key point is that state office is handed out for 'feeding' — and then you are free to do what you want. The feudal system of feeding under which the subordinate population was obliged to provide the Prince's locally appointed governor with a comfortable standard of living, supplying him with goods, and later money, was by no means a Russian invention, but it took very firm root in Russia, and is exceptionally tenacious, having successfully subverted the institution of private property, the institution of inheritance, and any concerns about a family's reputation. As soon as you rise to any public office, a genetic code begins to operate which dictates what is allowed and what is not allowed from then on, what you are entitled to take as a bureaucrat in a particular office. The public might moan, but they will eventually calm down, seeing a certain fairness in it all.

In the Soviet period a joke did the rounds in the Central Asian republics. They said that you could put a table in the public square in any village, place a red telephone on it, and a line of villagers would form, ready to give money to the person sitting behind it. Why? Just in case. Just because that's how it should be. Tradition. The story was that when a brigade from Russia came to Uzbekistan to investigate the 'cotton affair', the proud sons of the East simply could not comprehend what the brigade wanted from them. They could not understand what they were being accused of doing wrong. The investigator asked one of the accused whether he had given a bribe. The accused answered no to that, but confirmed that he had given money. Of course he had, because he had to, the man who he gave it to was respected by all. In other words the understanding which was ingrained in Central Asian culture about what was allowed and what wasn't differed fundamentally from what the Criminal Justice Code of the Soviet Union had to say on that point.

Sometimes it seems to me that in today's Russia you could place such a table with a fake hot line to the Kremlin in any village, or just in an open field, and a line of people holding envelopes full of cash would form in a flash. What else can we expect? That's just the times we live in, we don't know any other way. A special expression has even appeared: 'You need to duck and dive to get by.' And everyone ducks and dives, everyone is prepared to do a deal, everyone knows the part they have to play.

* * *

Speaking of the horrors of corruption, I think every one of us could write a whole treatise about this sad side of contemporary Russian life, equal in length to the collected works of Lev Nikolaevich Tolstoy. But I dare say that hardly anyone really thinks seriously about why it takes place. There is a very true saying, that all the millionaires in Russia are appointed by the state — and if someone is sent to work with natural resources he really does get very rich very quickly. But even if he is appointed as a billionaire, he is still *de facto* a public servant who goes to meetings with the president and prime minister, and carries out their wishes as if they were orders, and looks them in the face in the full knowledge that his fate and the fate of his riches depend above all on the authorities' attitude towards him. It turns out that the situation has not fundamentally changed since Tsarist times. But why does every citizen of our country decide at some point that it is in their best interests to serve the state?

Imagine a typical Russian citizen who suddenly decides to live honestly. He applied himself to his studies, say in the medical institute, and sincerely planned to live off his salary alone. And let's say he ends up in the regional hospital working as a doctor. If he is very lucky he ends up earning 12,000 a month, no more no less. 12, 000 rubles, that is. He'll work for a month or two on that salary. And then he'll get the bills. If he's lucky he lives in a flat left him by his parents, or with his parents, but he still has to pay for the gas, lighting, and water. But if, heaven forbid, he rents his apartment then he can forget about travelling to work on public transport or in his own car — he will have to walk — and feeding himself is impossible; he simply won't have enough money to buy his food.

Aleksandr Pochinok, who was at the time a minister, once came on my program. I asked if he had seen the standard consumer shopping basket which he recommended — it was certainly worth seeing. For those who are not aware, the standard consumer's shopping basket allows every Russian to go to the cinema once a year, and to buy two pairs of shoes — one for summer, one for winter. Women have it a bit better — they can allow themselves the incredible luxury of two bras per year, whereas men of course have none at all. Men, it's true to say, aren't too worried about that, but a look at the list, which allows for one change of overcoat in seven years, doesn't give great cause for joy.

But the food basket is another matter altogether. When I learned that each Russian citizen was allowed to eat a maximum of half an egg per day, I made breakfast accordingly, and offered it to Mr Pochinok. His response was the he doesn't eat much, and it was enough for him. And so then I understood the principle used to put together the food basket in Russia. It's true that this was announced by the same person who, whilst on a trip to one of the overseas business forums, beckoned his colleagues with the words, 'quickly, quickly come here I've found a shop where you can buy amazing wine at a very reasonable price — $1,500 per bottle.' That's how it always is in Russia, one man's trash is another man's treasure.

If we take a systematic approach to the question, we reach a conclusion which at first appears paradoxical. There is in fact no corruption in Russia. The thing is that when the whole population takes part in some process, then it can't be seen as something strange or alien — it's natural. So in our case we are just dealing with the appointment of people to positions for 'feeding'. The person placed in a particular position is given a license to use it to feed. Every Russian citizen who ends up working in government immediately finds himself in an interesting position. He sees that everyone around him is living well, despite their salaries being so small. What's more, they really don't live badly at all, and their salaries really are small by most standards. How is this possible? If we look at the clothes worn by members of the government, at their haircuts, their cars and gadgets, their watches, then it's quite obvious that they could never have bought them on their salaries. But it's out of the question to ask them, bluntly, what's going on guys? They wouldn't even understand what you were talking about, what the problem is.

The thing is that each of them is wearing several hats, so to speak. At the same time as performing their official duties in the government, they are manager of some state structure, which is operating entirely legally in the same market which they regulate. Let's take the example of Transport Minister Igor Evgenevich Levitin. Nothing could surprise him. He can't see that it's difficult to compete in a market where he is simultaneously the regulator and one of the main players. No, he thinks that this is entirely OK. There are well known cases when foreign partners were shocked by how Igor Evgenevich, visiting, began to openly lobby the interests of various airlines and airports, so that his opposite numbers were forced to ask outright what capacity he was speaking in. A question which surprised Mr Minister. It didn't occur to him that it was possible for him to speak in any other capacity, he was the Minister after all.

CHAPTER 2

The phenomenon of the interpenetration of officialdom and business was most vividly realized in the Moscow city government, which rightly held the leader's prize among all the Russian regions for corruption, and actually created an entirely new approach to it. Nine days before the appearance of President Medvedev's order dismissing Yuri Mikhailovich Luzhkov, *Novaya Gazeta* newspaper published a document which claimed that in 2004 the Moscow government had received a letter from the NTV TV station and taken the decision to sell an apartment to this author, using the Moscow city bureau of technical inventory price. I can say that it was a pretty expensive price for that year, and in any case quite different to the prices which were set on the city real estate monopoly. OK, the Moscow government gave up its share in the flat, but the flat was certainly not free of charge. The flat which was offered to me for purchase was just a concrete box, which would require three times as much spending on it to make it habitable than the builders had spent building the block it was in.

The article was really dirty and straight to the point — I was even quite touched. It said nothing about how the Moscow government had gifted large numbers of flats, town houses, and whole districts to people who, after Luzhkov's removal, lauded him as a torch bearer of democracy. Lots of leading journalists, media and cultural figures got free flats, workshops, studios, theaters, in return for which they were ready to defend Yuri Mikhailovich to the last. But I didn't like the article, so I decided to find out what was going on, and tried to get in touch with Luzhkov. I didn't have his direct phone number, so I just called his office.

Imagine my surprise when Luzhkov said that he would like to meet with me. Just a few hours later I was in the mayor's office. What I saw amazed me. Normally there was a ceaseless buzz outside Luzhkov's office, crowds of people who wanted an audience with the great man. I say great because Yuri Mikhailovich's powers, and most importantly his image were such that one could say that his ego loomed over Moscow, eclipsing even Tsereteli's statue of Peter the Great. But this time there was no one waiting outside Luzhkov's office. Everyone who had just the day before been eating out of Luzhkov's hand had fled, sensing impending trouble.

I entered the office. There was a copy of *Novaya Gazeta* on Yuri Mikhailovich's desk. He began by assuring me that he had not had anything to do with the article, that he was not to blame for it. And then we talked at length about what was going on in the city. It was then that I realized that Luzhkov really did not understand — did not understand at all — what was going on, and how the system which had been set up with his direct involvement worked. He had completely lost touch with reality. He really didn't know about the endless bribes which were needed to get building permits. Or how many years it took to get them. Or how any tender, whatever for, always ended with the pre-planned outcome. He didn't inquire how his deputies — like Resin for example — had watches worth millions, and not just one of them. He was not surprised at all by their high standard of living. At some point he had really begun to believe all the eulogies which were uttered by those whose fate could be decided at any moment by a change in his mood. If Luzhkov liked you — then you were a billionaire. If Luzhkov was removed — then your life was over.

* * *

At one point Luzhkov had summed up his view — a capitalist approach to work, but with a socialist approach to re-distribution. I can't say whether he succeeded in applying that, but during his time he created what was basically a geriocratic system of government, resembling in many respects the Soviet Politburo. But that was only half the story — he created a system which in the end devoured him as well. Every toady and lickspittle was given his share, and they gorged themselves to their fill. Every Moscow district head felt like the head of a separate state in which this remarkable system flourished. There was not a single area of activity which worked simply and efficiently. Everywhere one could find front companies in one form or another. I'm leaving aside the highly lucrative construction business, in which the mayor and his courtiers were the main players. And Vladimir Iosifovich Resin, who just like the abovementioned Minister Levitin was totally confused about whether he was the regulator of a market — or its owner.

The incomes of these people involved figures which were so large that they lost all comprehension of what money was. For them, it just became more pieces of paper. Expensive cars, villas all around the world, businesses in Russia and overseas which they managed with complete inefficiency — it made no difference to them anyway. A completely different mode of existence. They were placed in these positions by the system and were taking advantage of the opportunities to 'feed'.

Yurii Bulanov, head of the southern city district who was arrested in 2010 and convicted of embezzlement simply could not understand what he had done wrong. OK, the land had been bought by companies associated with him. OK, some houses had been built on it. But it had all been done officially. What exactly was he was guilty of?

One can perhaps understand why he reacted this way — for many years he had worked under Petr Biryukov, who up until then had been deputy mayor, and whom the new city government was in no hurry to dismiss. And Mr Biryukov's apartment is situated in a building which belongs to Bulanov. And what's so bad about the fact that the son of the former district head managed the very same company which provided municipal services in that district, and which had received funds to carry out major repairs of the housing there? After all, he's an experienced specialist in that field, why not? So what if his firms work ineffectively — who is effective these days? What's the difference if Bulanov's wife got government money to carry out a series of essential cultural events for the city and district. What's so bad about that? She's a talented events manager. Just like Luzhkov's wife — she's a talented businesswoman, is she not?

She is indeed. I met Elena Nikolaevna (Luzhkov) several times — she really is a very clever woman. And the Inteko business was not just the biggest in Moscow — there were branches and subsidiaries in other regions of Russia. But then again, even a child can comprehend that if you have a business, and you've got the mayor of Moscow behind you, then you won't have any problems opening a branch in a another town — someone will always be ready to do business with you. Mayor of Moscow is a major political office, after all. Of course that doesn't mean that Inteko was not successful in its own right! Although it must be said that as soon as Luzhkov left office, this talented businesswoman could do nothing more than stand by and watch how, despite all her talents, her business was taken over by new owners. The question which I cannot answer is whether Yuri Mikhailovich was really so naive as to believe that his wife would be allowed to continue to expand her business when he left office? And another question which I can't answer is why does no one study history? After all, in Russia it never happens as Luzhkov seemed to believe it would. In Russia we have the system for 'feeding'.

* * *

When the moment of truth arrived, and it became clear that Inteko had acquired a large amount of land which it couldn't pay for, wicked tongues said that Luzhkov did his wife's bidding and saved her business by buying up plots of land for crazy amounts of money. But Luzhkov's supporters argued that this was a simplistic view. Inteko, they said, was a large company, and a large number of unfortunate people were waiting in line for flats which they had already paid for to be built. Their interests had to be looked after — these were the interests of the Russian people after all!

After all, in Russia the interests of the people are always the top priority. Just as when the homes in the Rechnik settlement were demolished, and their inhabitants literally thrown out onto the freezing streets, when the houses in Yuzhnoye Butovo were pulled down to build yet more concrete blocks of flats, and the mayor accused the Prokofiev family of being louts for refusing to move, and when the speaker of the Moscow city assembly Mr Platonov came and asked if the interests of Muscovites meant nothing and couldn't some flexibility be shown. In all these cases, it was of course undeniable that the people's interests were being defended. One can hear the clear echo of Soviet thinking in all of this, and Luzhkov and his team were clearly influenced by it. Imagining themselves to be the embodiment of the state's interests, they thought that they actually were both the state and the people, and that no law of private property existed or could ever exist. All that existed was their right to decide what belonged to whom.

Right in the center of the airport in the Japanese town of Narit there is a little house, just a hut really, with a tiny plot of land around it, surrounded by runways. The owner of the house, an elderly gentleman, had refused to sell it. Just outright refused. He had been offered as much money as he wanted. And then some more. But every time he stubbornly refused, because there was no way he was going to lose his home. His forefathers had lived there, his children had grown up there, and this where he wanted to spend the rest of his life. And how do you think the story ended? You won't believe it. No heavy mob came. There was no fire to burn the house down. No Mr Platonov came with disapproving words. No Luzhkov came running, shouting that the old man was a lout. No one offered him a charming new one-bedroomed flat on Akhmad Kadyrov street. No, the airport was built around the little house — and the planes had to fly round it!

Sounds funny, but that is what private property is all about. No one played on feelings of guilt, asking if private interests were being put before public ones. An argument which is anyway entirely degenerate. What does it mean to say that private interests are above public ones? It's just private property, full stop. No one can simply take it, even if they really want to. If you want to have it, you have to pay for it.

In Russia the question of private property doesn't even arise — who respects it as an institution anyway? Only in the realms of wishful thinking. Your home may be dear to you — but no one gives a damn if the people need it. Just give up your ramshackle old house — and you'll get a decent flat in return! Don't bother arguing that you will never move into that flat because it's impossible to make it habitable. No one cares about that. Don't bother pointing out that it was Moscow city government which set the fashion for building apartment blocks without gas and electricity — you have to pay crazy sums of money to have them connected, but the flats are deemed ready for habitation all the same. And the young families with prams and little children have to get to the ninth floor by foot. Nothing wrong with that!

And you'll be told that there is no corruption going on here at all. They just had to find some homes for Muscovites. No one is guilty of doing anything wrong. How can anyone by guilty, if all these people are doing their jobs so well. Vladimir Iosifovich Resin, for example, is a top class professional. Normally it takes many years to get planning permission. But you want to get it quicker? And why exactly?

These people wrapped themselves in procedures, and officially they abided by the majority of laws. After all, there is no law in Russia forbidding married couples from working in the same organization. And the former head of the southern administrative district of Moscow was by no means an exception — if we look at the staff lists and work out who is related, then it becomes clear that there are many wives and children who are very happy working in organizations which operate in sectors of the economy which are regulated by their husbands and fathers. So what? Should people be removed from their jobs over such trifles? Let's take the example of the former head of the Moscow Metro, Dmitry Gaev, who apparently owned the patent for the metro's travel card system. A real technical genius. Is there anything wrong with the fact that his son ran the company which produced the magnetic cards used to pay for travel, and his daughter had the exclusive contract for sale of souvenirs using the logo of the metro? How long did it take to work out that, to put it mildly, there was something not quite right with this situation, and to remove Gaev from his position and begin an investigation.

* * *

During that memorable discussion with Luzhkov, I asked him whether he could not see that all around him everyone was on the take. Even his wife Elena Nikolaevna had told me with horror that in order to get a permit to build something she had to pay bribes. The system didn't care what words were written on the document, the devil was, as ever, in the detail. It was well known that in Moscow a visit to the mayor still decided nothing, what was important was what color ink had been used to write the decision. And you still had to go through the seven circles of hell and make sure to humbly thank everyone at every level, otherwise there would be trouble. No one would actually block you, but nothing would get moving. Of course, you could try to get by without corruption, without paying anyone off, and you might, in theory, get somewhere. You just might.

Luzhkov created a system which the other Russian regions were happy to take and adapt to their needs. Its key element was the blatant, provocative and arrogant involvement of the city administration in commercial activities. The system was simple — only the city was both the regulator and a participant in the process. Just give the city its fair share. And if you gave a share of the apartments you were building to the city, then the city would decide whom to give them to. The city wins, because in this way it regulates the housing market and the players on the market. The city becomes the main commercial player, deciding who gets what land to rent and at what rate, and plots of land of equal market value can end up costing very different amounts of money. Or the city's share in different projects can vary. How can we speak of fair competition if the costs are unequal for different players right from the start?

A unique situation had come about in the building industry in Moscow. To this day it is impossible to work out who is building what within Moscow's administrative borders. Under Luzhkov, the number of genuine professionals got smaller and smaller year by year. More and more people came into the industry who had a very tenuous link to building. If we are to believe the words of the famous businessman Shalva Chigirinsky, he became a successful property developer in Moscow only by giving half of his business, under an unwritten agreement, to the Moscow city administration. And when, on my TV show *To The Barrier*, I asked the former head of the development company Mirax Group Sergey Polonsky whether he had paid any money to the Moscow city government in order to receive building permission, Polonsky froze, fixed me with a stare, and refused to answer. After that incident, it's true, he wrote in his articles and books that TV programs like *To The Barrier* should be closed for good. That's why it is always so touching to see these duped shareholders — you want to ask them who it was that unexpectedly invaded the market? Were they strangers, those people who suddenly conned you? Righteous anger would look a bit different. You want to ask them how much money they got for letting the crooks enter the market in the first place.

At some point it became clear that it wasn't even necessary to sell apartments. If it suited you could sell an empty concrete box at an astronomical price. All attempts to work out the real costs of building these magnificent edifices were unsuccessful. You could be forgiven for thinking that the apartment blocks were being constructed by English lords, using golden trowels to lay the cement, which was mixed from diamond dust. But if you went to any building site, you could see the faces of workers from Central Asia, and you could quite easily determine that the quality of the building work was very low. There is clearly some sort of con hidden somewhere here. Meanwhile the very concept of cheap apartments completely disappeared from Moscow.

It became clear that it was necessary to pay the city crazy sums of money for something which was in reality none of the city's business. It turned out that the city authorities thought themselves to be the *de facto* owners of the land. Not the Muscovites. The official explanation sounded very well-meaning; some of the flats would go to the city, to be given to those in need. But to be honest I never understood who would actually get them. Judging by the amount of building going on, it seemed that half of Moscow should be living in flats handed out by the Moscow government under social security programs. But nothing of the sort happened or ever will — there could never be any question of some sort of mass hand-out of flats. What was really going on, in all likelihood, was some sort of obscure deal with the federal authorities, cultural figures and the media who got free flats in the city to keep them happy. There were even three payment levels, most probably indicating proximity to the city administration. In any case, it doesn't make any sense to talk about a real market — it simply did not exist.

Moreover, the apartments were bought and sold by organizations with direct links to the Moscow government. And no one was surprised by this. Whole departments used the state unitary enterprise system to get up to all manner of things, imaging themselves to be entrepreneurs, despite lacking the professional and personal attributes to do so successfully. This approach killed healthy competition for good. Just imagine, there was a state unitary enterprise which run the car parking system in Moscow. What exactly is car parking in Moscow? Nothing to speak of, just a piece of asphalt marked up with some paint. A person walks up and down in a pseudo-military uniform and collects money from car owners because their cars are parked on that asphalt. But this state unitary enterprise made a loss. It might be impossible to comprehend that it made a loss — but it did. Sounds like a bad joke, but that's really how it was.

The Moscow government contained departments which should have logically been subordinated to the federal government. It's hard to find a sensible reason why the mayoralty was involved with road building. But it was, and big time. Turns out that the prices per kilometer were completely crazy, and just as in the case of house building they bore no relationship to the real costs involved. On what basis was their value established? Maybe on the basis that someone wanted to make lots of money?

As we well know, road building in Russia is a goldmine. According to the findings of the Federal Audit Office, we know that during his time in office Transport Minister Igor Levitin managed to build less than 200 kilometers of federal roads, at the average price of 41 million dollars per kilometer. Funny, but Moscow beat these figures many times over, and I'm sure they got great satisfaction from knowing that. According to rumor there was a whole department which somehow managed to justify this and get great satisfaction from it.

When Vladimir Resin was asked how the commercial value per kilometer of Moscow's roads was determined, the answer he gave was astounding. It turned out that the mayoralty had to buy up plots of land! No surprise that the company ACT, which belonged to the notorious businessman Telman Ismailov, took the city administration to court demanding compensation, because the company had built warehouses on the plots of land where the road was due to be built, and these now had to be pulled down. In essence this is the same as the well-known con from the age of railroad construction in America: the Moscow government handed out long-term leases on the plots of land where the roads would eventually be built to affiliated organizations.

It turned out that the city administration was embroiled in the most outlandish of projects. For example, when Shalva Chigirinsky became co-owner of Moscow oil processing plant, the city government got a share in the British company Sibir Energy. You would be forgiven for asking what bearing this had on the lives of Moscow's citizens. The city unexpectedly stuck its paw into the purchase of Vnukovo airport and a fleet of aircraft, which it had no idea how to manage — and which it was not even permitted to manage. There is no doubt that when the road to Sheremetevo airport was shut, completely unexpectedly and with no prior declaration of warfare, the airport managers took this as the direct machinations of their competitor, with the aim of winning over their clients for Vnukovo airport. And it's hard not to agree with them, since it is the city which takes the decision about repairing roads, and the city was suffering because Vnukovo was badly managed. But how could Vnukovo possibly be well managed, if the city doesn't know how to manage anything anyway?

Not only did Luzhkov create a unique system for getting all his buddies involved in profitable commercial activities, the joy of it all was that this was entirely blatant. I would even go as far as saying that there was a kind of charm to it. It was considered entirely normal to visit the mayor of Moscow and ask for his help with whatever you wanted to do. The degree of Yuri Mikhailovich's personal involvement in the sad history of Cherkizovsky market was such that he did not balk at turning up on the market owner's birthday and joyfully proclaiming: 'Telman, you are our friend and brother, today is the most important of days for us!' Which in itself would of course not be so bad, if we could be sure that the contribution of the market to the budget was at all significant.

The system of front companies operated completely openly and no one seemed to be annoyed about it. If it's in line with the law, then all's well and good, they would say. All the more so if they pay their taxes. For example, the city administration was directly involved in one of the first gambling operations in existence in the city. No great surprise that a variety of low-level city officials and organizations associated with them, having got the gambling bug, are in no hurry to do anything about the renamed Vulkan lottery clubs and other dodgy establishments. They need to put food on the table every day after all! They were placed in these positions to 'feed', and how could anything else be expected of them? They were given their patch to feed from, and that is exactly what they are doing.

In classical economic theory, three basic factors of production are identified: labor, land and capital. Since all the land, at least within the boundaries of the city of Moscow, was subject to the whims of Luzhkov, he personally decided who could be successful, and who could not. Who could flourish, and who couldn't. It reached absurd levels; the official value of the stalls operating at bus stops in the city amounted to no more than a few kopecks. However, one fine moment they were all let out to structures affiliated with one of the most senior members of the Moscow city administration. And these structures then concluded new rent agreements with the unfortunate stall-holders at astronomical prices. And this was all entirely legal! No one was doing anything wrong.

CHAPTER 3

The approach described in the previous chapter is applied to every type of economic activity which may present any kind of interest. And every single Russian official is convinced that it is entirely legitimate for him to wear several hats at the same time. In order to identify the origins of this phenomenon, let's have a look at some fairly recent history.

If you take a look at the pay department of any government organization and at the wages of the officials, you might think that you're in Wonderland. In the Soviet period this was easy to explain — the official salary scale set a maximum wage limit for the typical worker, and the wages of ministers, the secretaries of the Party Central Committee, the members of the Politburo and others did not significantly exceed that limit — perhaps by two or three times at the most. But at the same time everyone was fully aware that in times of deficit, when it was practically impossible to buy many essential products, one and the same ruble could have an entirely different purchasing power for different categories of citizen. With one ruble you could buy two blocks of ice-cream, a bottle of wine, half a stick of sausage — but at the same time that one ruble could be incredibly valuable — the official rate of exchange was 61 kopecks to the dollar — and in some places like the notorious 200th department of the GUM state supermarket, or the special network of 'Berezka' shops you could buy shortage goods at prices which couldn't be found anywhere else.

People who came from abroad got their salaries in so called checks or vouchers with different serial numbers depending on which countries they came from. All of these checks allowed you to buy goods in hard currency shops, but depending on the serial number, you would be entitled to a different selection of goods, and the prices for one and the same product would vary — meaning that some were a bit out of some people's league. I recall that half the country got rations of different types of food products and household goods on top of their salaries. A system came into being where despite the official absence of a large difference in wage levels, there was a huge difference in the real value of those wages. What came about was in essence, if not a corruption scheme, then certainly a classical system of 'feeding'. Just as in Tsarist times, the inhabitant of the socialist system clearly understood that depending on where he was positioned in the social hierarchy, he could count on certain kinds of perks. In fact, as he climbed the career ladder, he would receive a certain piece of territory for 'feeding' and the state would tell him openly exactly what kind of income he could expect from it.

Some time ago my father-in-law, on return from a long foreign posting, was entitled to purchase a Volga car. The official state prices for cars were set very high, but even at these high prices it was virtually impossible to buy a small car — you had to wait several years in line. It was still possible to buy a car second-hand, although it would be crazily overpriced. So, my father-in-law wanted a black Volga, but it turned out to be impossible to get hold of one. The retailer said no way, the black ones were only for members of the Party Central Committee — you can buy a cherry-colored one. In other words, even such apparently insignificant questions were very strictly regulated.

The system worked perfectly. Thanks to the established order of things, everyone knew that if someone came along dressed in expensive clothes, it was either a responsible worker, who had achieved a certain professional standing, or a speculator, who could be arrested and thrown into prison. Every official was very well informed about what he could expect to get through his position at work, and what he would get after a few years if he were promoted, but he also knew that if he got the sack, despite all his hard work he would literally end up on the street without the shirt on his back.

Once the country jumped unexpectedly from socialism to a modern market system, it became clear that the state could no longer deliver the raft of welfare services which it had inherited, but the hypocrisy which had become typical of the Soviet authorities in the end of the 1980's and early 1990s easily survived into the new era. Officially the ministers and other officials earned kopecks, but in reality they lived quite splendidly. Bright young things thronged around every important official, running various commercial schemes, not neglecting their own wellbeing while they were at it. Once again there were clear rules of the game — if you were a deputy minister, you were entitled to a certain class of suits, watches, cars, and holidays in certain resorts, if you were a minister, commensurate with your grade you could expect goods and services a class higher, and if you managed to reach the very top, then who cares — do what you want!

Attempts to break this system came up against opposition from all quarters, even from the lowest levels. The thing was that within the state enterprises there was a very attractive scheme for handing out travel packages and so-called goods orders, and to this day even the canteen prices compare favorably with the prices in other public eateries, even if these are situated 100 meters from the places where our public servants work. You might frown skeptically — surely this isn't big money? Yes, but it's still money — it's all money.

* * *

From time to time one hears different opinions about how one might improve the situation. Vladimir Volfovich Zhirinovsky, for example, once suggested legalizing bribes and collecting taxes from them. Such ideas aren't as silly as they may seem, but they are still impossible to implement. Even the size of a bribe plays no role. After all, what's important is not how much you pay in order to get something done. What's important is the system itself — that you understand that you are obliged to 'pay your share'. The principle, once wryly formulated by Yeltsin's economic advisor Livshits, that big business had to learn to share their profits by paying taxes to government, has taken on a completely different meaning. It turns out that you still need to pay your share even when there is no justification for doing so.

The anti-corruption measures which are typically proposed, involving the removal of officials from decision-making positions and jobs where they have responsibility for overseeing certain key procedures, sound rather fantastical. What do they really amount to? They mean that we would need to tell a whole army of people that they are no longer needed. But then what is the point of trained professionals, if they don't have to take any decisions? In this case the function they perform is just a fiction, and we can easily do without it.

What's more, how can you explain to untold numbers of people employed in government offices that they have to disappear, as if by miracle, and get nothing in return for doing so. Of course they'll ask what's in it for them. No surprise that whenever talk starts of staff reductions in a given ministry, a whole pile of federal agencies appears at the same level in the hierarchy, where all the former employees end up, with new assistants and subordinates — and all still working for the state. Aleksandr Pochinok once came up with a half serious rule, whereby every reform which was aimed at reducing the numbers of bureaucrats in Russia would result in their numbers growing 1.5 times. If we apply that rule to publically available statistics, it turns out that by around 2040 there will only be public officials left in Russia. And then we will have to stop talking about corruption, because it's impossible to corrupt yourself. We will end up with a complex and pervasive system of 'feeding'.

As I have already said, the official salaries which public officials get are strictly based on the unified salary scale, which is tied to the minimum wage. The proposed system of incentives and awards, which are supposed to identify the best staff, need to be clearly and simply defined — who exactly are the best? And do we need them in any case? When the staff themselves have to decide who is the best among them, it normally ends up working the tried and tested way. Yes, we will pick someone, they say, but then that person has to share the bonus money with those who selected them — or the top management needs to be paid off.

And speaking of selecting the best staff, can you really say, hand on heart, that in the absence of objective criteria your wife, a female relative or lover would not seem undeniably better than a cold distant stranger who happens to be working under you? The wisdom taken from Russian classical literature, that it is natural to want to do a favor for a family member, rings true to this day. No surprise then that in recent years the dream of a large number of Russians is not to become a businessman — not even to become the oligarch Abramovich — but, much better than that, to become a state official. The embodiment of all that is good on this earth is seen to lie in this proximity to power.

Indeed, if we take a look at the fleet of cars belonging to Russian state officials, it becomes very clear why no one dreams of becoming a businessman. Why would they want to hassle for every kopeck and rack their brains about how to submit their accounts without incurring fines and losses, when they could become a bureaucrat, who has no responsibility for anything, makes no decisions, and, in Russia's current economy, is never likely to be seriously punished for anything he does wrong. And you can treat yourself to a lifestyle of luxury that others could not dream of. If the official carefully abides by the rules of the game, then his hands are pretty much free in everything else he does. Whatever sin he commits, however terrible, he is somehow saved by a golden parachute, to land in a pre-prepared diplomatic role. And even if he doesn't get that diplomatic job, he will get some other cozy position.

* * *

Let's now recall what happened in Russia at the turn of the century, when Putin came to power and announced the start of a counter-revolution against the oligarchs.

Obviously he came to power with his entourage. And this entourage obviously expected to be rewarded in some way. Obviously, this reward was in the form of top positions in the government. But it was also clear that the oligarchs could not be trusted, so it was essential to give oversight over the distribution of resources to people who could be. So for that reason, large numbers of commissars were posted into business structures, trusted people whose task was to keep an eye on the national wealth and make sure that political interests were being protected. A number of these commissars were simultaneously working on government business — and continue to do so. These people suddenly found themselves members of the boards of directors of various companies, chairmen of oversight committees, and they could be seen as *de facto* representatives of state interests within the main tax-paying organizations of the Russian Federation — in other words, they were the 'watchers'. The phrase which any American will utter with pride, I pay you taxes, and you live off them, does not apply at all in Russia. I would go so far as to say that even if all the citizens of Russia stopped paying their taxes, then this wouldn't have an impact on government finances, since the natural resources monopolies are anyway the main tax payers in the country.

But as soon as these people took on roles in the economy and started carrying out the work entrusted to them, they began to ask whether this work was just an 'optional subject'. OK, let's say it really was optional, and they got nothing for it — or say five kopecks — their questioning gazes would still ask what they would get in return — they were giving up their personal time, and expected to be shown some gratitude for it.

And of course gratitude had to be shown. And not only in the form of hard cash, but in the beginning simply in the form of an understanding that our guys, decent guys, who certainly aren't our enemies, could be entrusted with government money, competitions, tenders and other such activities, and that the profit could be directed towards funding complex political structures.

Nevertheless, we are still basically talking about political appointees, who have been allowed to use the full potential of commercial organizations in order to solve a range of political problems — and here Putin's approach was exactly the right one. But this approach also had clear faults and drawbacks. It's important to acknowledge that in the years which have passed since the establishment of market relations in Russia, the foundations of respect for market relations have not been laid. Neither under Gorbachev nor under Yeltsin. However many slogans were deployed, private property remained a highly contested concept — in fact the idea of private property is something of a joke if judges in the pay of the oligarchs can take the last kopeck off a man if that is what their rich masters order.

And so Putin's friends within the system became notorious. We can only stand by and rejoice at how well they are doing, as we watch the colossal growth of their personal fortunes. When Vladimir Vladimirovich (Putin) said in an interview to three federal TV stations that the goal was not simply to be able to sack a minister, but to make him work, this clearly reflected one of the strengths of his approach, although at some point it also became a weakness.

Loyalty to friends, the ability to forgive mistakes, a passionate desire to make the team work, all these are undoubtedly positive qualities. Furthermore, Putin is certainly not a vengeful person. Khodorkovsky's allies may beg to differ, but I will give an example which proves my case. As much as Yakovlev's behavior raised doubts when Sobchak was being hounded, Putin never lowered himself by seeking personal revenge. I should say, by the way, that it is highly naive to say that the Khodorkovsky case was all about personal revenge. The current attempts to portray Khodorkovsky as some kind of saint or gentle lamb are a long way from the historical truth, and efforts to position him in the democratic camp are entirely fantastical. At least when Mikhail Borisovich (Khodorkovsky) was still free his stated political views didn't give the slightest impression that he was a democrat.

Putin's loyalty to his friends and his sincere desire to make people work effectively often lead to unwanted outcomes, because unfortunately Putin's friends often do him no favors at all. A good example was Aleksey Leonidovich Kudrin's behavior during a visit to Washington in the fall of 2011, when he made some critical comments to journalists about the government which had just been formed and his desire or otherwise to work in it — this was clearly insubordination, and a breach of discipline. This challenge and the subsequent public spat with President Medvedev put Prime Minister Putin in a very difficult position, as he had to choose between the national interest and his personal loyalties. But in such matters Putin's choice is always clear and unambiguous, so it was quite easy to predict how he would reacted to these events.

One can also recall the long friendship between Vladimir Vladimirovich and General Viktor Cherkesov and his wife, and conclude that after the harsh conflict between Cherkesov, Nikolai Patrushev and Sergey Ivanov, Putin demonstrated the wisdom of Solomon, since everyone lost their jobs. As these events unfolded, the new positions which the protagonists got, based on the specific circumstances of the time, were not of equal standing or significance. It was clear that Putin was not seeking personal revenge, and not trying to get at opponents or allies who had at some point taken the liberty of making public statements which could have put him in a difficult position. But alas the ability of Putin's friends to take responsibility for their actions often falls tragically short of Putin's own level of personal responsibility — Putin's friends seem to think that their friendship with him brings just privileges, and no obligations.

CHAPTER 4

An important point which we should never let out of sight is that the feudal principle of 'feeding' will always come into conflict with the principles of capitalism, which uphold the inviolability of private property. They are in fact two opposing systems. After rejecting socialism, Russian society had to get used to living in a complex, multidimensional new legal environment. The State Duma had to pass new laws to protect private property and establish organs which in turn had oversight over these laws — in other words, the courts. Of course, there had always been courts in Russia. But at no time before had such a large volume of work fallen to them, and at no time before had their activities been under such close scrutiny.

And what did this scrutiny reveal? It revealed that in Russia such a thing as the legal system should not be left to its own devices. It's a good thing that Anglo-Saxon law does not operate in Russia — heaven forbid that the rule of precedent should begin to apply here, that would be terrible! That would mean that a decision taken, for example, somewhere in Khanty-Mansiysk, however much money it cost to influence the court, or however wrong it might be, would end up being law in the rest of Russia. That wouldn't do at all. In Russia two completely identical cases can result in two completely different court rulings. And there is no point in trying to find any logic in it — it's better to try and find the real reason behind it.

The people who started all this back in the 1990s were those bright young things, later to be known as the oligarchs, who sauntered round Russia helping themselves to the tastiest morsels of state property. Realizing the power of court decisions, they took wide advantage of the absence of precedent, buying up everything lock stock and barrel. So any attempt to win a court case against the notorious Yukos on the same patch where Yukos was the main player was completely hopeless — and the same applies to a court case on Lukoil's patch, the list goes on and on. The situation became quite absurd — the arbitrage courts had individual judges who specialized in working for specific commercial organizations. And of course the success rate of these organizations was remarkably high.

By the end of Boris Yeltsin's presidency, the oligarchs had their paws all over the court system. At some point the Kremlin realized that they would need to tackle this, since with this state of affairs it was impossible to impose order on the country. A genuinely independent court system was needed. But in Russia one form of slavery is often followed by another, and only then does the system become genuinely free.

It's clear that when Putin came to power and began to tackle the corruption which was widespread amongst most court staff, he could only trust those people who in academician Sakharov's words were the model of incorruptibility — the representatives of the law enforcement agencies. So a large number of staff, who had already reached the rank of general, were delegated to the Presidential Administration with the sole aim of overseeing the court system. It was clear that they could impose their will only by influencing the thinking of individual judges. But the challenge of working with these judges was that even if the chairman of the court or the head of the court administration knew what the position of the government was, it might still make no difference. The oligarchs, knowing no shame, paid such crazy sums of money to their pet judges, that blatantly biased and illegal decisions were passed contrary even to the will of the Kremlin.

Despite all this, the respect for the legal system was such that it was not possible just to subject it to some form of punishment.

It was essential to take into account the fact that the judges were completely overloaded with work. The scale of disorder in the country was such that even at the end of the 1990s and beginning of 2000 it was necessary to pay between five and ten thousand dollars just to get a case before a particular judge. No surprise therefore that even the administrative workers of the court accumulated impressive sums of money, and anyone who could take advantage of the 'feeding' opportunities provided by the position of judge immediately became very rich — simply by virtue of this position. The money would simply pour into his pockets. And as we know tricking computer systems is a national sport in Russia.

When it comes to the court system, the mind boggles at the sums of money which were involved. At one time I reported to Putin just how far the situation had gone. Lawyers could be divided into two categories — the first knew whom to talk to, and the second category knew how much money had to be paid. All the rest of it — legal argument and knowledge of the law was of secondary importance. Of course, this refers to the headline cases, but it was those cases which played a determining role.

* * *

So it was necessary to take active measures to tackle this biased and corrupt system. The aim was to create a counterbalance to the financial power of the oligarchs and criminals, in the form of appointments at various levels by the Presidential Administration.

In the place of the oligarchs came the state, which through iron determination managed to seize the initiative, creating, with varying degrees of success, a system of administrative subordination under the Presidential Administration. But then the time-honored national tradition took over, and the state officials began to confuse their own interests with state interests, just like in the classic Soviet comedies. They would of course be happy to carry out state functions, but the state consisted of so many different people, that it was easy to get mixed up. And then you began to think that you really do personally embody the state. You are a member of the Presidential Administration, after all. So why not start to promote your own interests, rather than just those of the state?

And so it ended up that the Presidential Administration began to play a major role in the fate of the court personnel. It was the members of the Presidential Administration who came along with serious faces and explained what was recommended and not recommended to do, and they determined which judges got promoted, and who got the awards. And then another important aspect of all this became clear. It turned out that the judges were working to several different masters. I certainly don't mean goddess of law Themis — she who, as we known, has to keep her eyes covered. The judges turned out to be highly susceptible both to the will of the members of the Presidential Administration, and to the regional leaders. The Moscow city administration, for example, learned how to get on marvelously with the judges in Moscow, setting an example which the other federal regions sought to emulate. It was no secret that the Moscow mayoralty topped up the judges' wages through a system of 'Luzhkov bonuses'. What kind of independent court system could we hope for if the city administration awarded these various pay incentives to the judges? Of course it would be silly to suggest that the Moscow administration could lose a case in any of the courts of Moscow. Who would bite the hand which fed them?

I myself encountered the joys of trying to fight the local authorities through the courts when the mayor of the city of Samara took me to court. The initial sum which the mayor sought was ten million rubles, the court case dragged out for nearly two years, and in conclusion the court ruled that I had to pay the mayor 70 thousand rubles. I was basically told that I had to hand over the money because the mayor felt offended. No need to apologize or to deny anything — they didn't claim that I had lied. But the mayor had reportedly been very offended by my words, so I had to hand over a bit of cash. The situation seemed so outlandish that I decided that I had only two possible courses of action — either to pay the money, or to use the money to buy some sweets and give them to the offended mayor, so that he wouldn't fuss and moan like a child. I had always thought that the purpose of a court was to determine the truth, rather than to indulge in open declarations of love towards the regional authorities.

Getting a position to 'feed' on a promising patch ensured that a pliable judge could have an exceptionally cozy existence — just as in the well-known case of Ludmila Maikova, whose coziness reached such levels that she simply lost all contact with reality. It's not hard to understand why. I can't be sure of the exact figures, but it seemed that thanks to Mrs Maikova sums of money changed hands which were equal to the budgets of large African states. Of course, when I dared to criticize her activities and her rulings, a whole crowd of ardent fans rose up in support not just of her personally but of her unique skills as a judge. And the nature of these skills was that certain business groups had an unprecedented degree of success in the courts cases which they were involved in. And at the same time Mrs Maikova did pretty well for herself, and the other judges were not doing badly either, and the Moscow city government was also taking a decent share.

The chronology of events is interesting and quite illuminating. In August 2004 Ludmila Nikolaevna (Maikova) acquired an apartment and an underground parking space in the residential complex at Sparrow Hills, from a company which had frequently figured as one of the parties in cases before her court, and the cost of the apartment was reduced by almost 700 thousand dollars. At the same time Mrs Maikova made a complaint about her living conditions to the Moscow city government, and requested that she be provided with separate apartments for herself and for her 23 year old daughter. The city government obliged her by passing an order, giving an apartment to Ludmila Nikolaevna, and another to her daughter. In other words, two new apartments asides from the home she already had. The judge vacated her apartment on Ostashkovskaya Street, and in return got more spacious accommodation in a new building on Michurinsky Prospect, and a separate apartment for her daughter near the Shchukinskaya metro station. The paperwork was made out as an exchange with an additional payment on top, for a sum, which while not purely symbolic, was not as big as one might have expected. Moreover, according to the papers filed in the financial department of the Moscow city government, the payment was made by a certain commercial bank under the instructions of Mrs Maikova.

When I began to unravel this scam, Lydmila Ivanovna tried to explain her apartment deals in the pages of *Vedomosti* paper, claiming that the need to move to a new apartment arose when the case of Domodedovo airport's rent was being examined in the district arbitrage court. Pressure had allegedly been applied on her, and some unidentified persons had even intimidated her right by the entrance to her own home.

Turns out that Lyudmila Nikolaevna rushed to buy the new apartments out of fright! And it seems that her fright was so great that she even needed to buy several new apartments. I took the trouble of checking the records. The Domodedovo rent case was being examined by the Moscow District Federal Arbitrage Court at the beginning of 2004, and on the 10 March that court had already cancelled its decision and sent the case back to the court of first instance. But was the Domodedovo case the only one being examined at that time? No, the Moscow District Federal Arbitrage Court examines hundreds of cases at the same time. As the judge herself had said, she had been intimidated by unidentified persons. So why had it been necessary to link this directly to the Domodedovo case? And moreover, it remained unclear when the event near the entrance to her home had happened, and indeed whether it had happened at all. Maikova had basically indicated to her colleagues in the court system who was out of favor with her and needed to be 'wiped out'.

I will remind the reader that the apartment on Sparrow Hills had been bought in August 2004. The order of the Moscow city government regarding the other two apartments had come out in September. Turns out that that damned Domodedovo case had already been dealt with half a year previously! But Maikova insisted that she was in danger. She did in fact live in one of the less comfortable areas of Moscow — Ostashkovskaya Street was in the Medvedkovo district, near the Moscow circular road. And the Moscow city government, or more precisely Yuri Mikhailovich Luzhkov and Vladimir Iosifovich Resin personally gave her an apartment on Michurinsky prospect. A good district. A new block with a guarded perimeter. Perhaps it was not quite legal, but it was definitely generous. And definitely a safe apartment.

So you are probably thinking that Maikova would be in a hurry to move from her dangerous apartment to a safe one, so as to at last live free from fear. Certainly, a person whose life and health were really under threat would do exactly that. But the judge lived for another year and a half in the bad apartment, while the one at Sparrow Hills was being done up.

So she had been intimidated, and had lived in fear for half a year, but she still did nothing. She just carried on being scared, and carried on redecorating. She stubbornly stayed in the old, 'dangerous' apartment, stubbornly refused to move into the new, safer apartment, and heroically waits for the redecorating to be done in the third apartment she had bought. And finally, four months after the mayor gave her the safe apartment on Michurinsky, Maikova puts it up for sale, without having lived a single day there herself. Nice!

I wonder if a normal citizen who had been unfortunate enough to be intimidated near the entrance to his house, could get almost five hundred square meters of real estate in the form of three or four gifted apartments in return for his frayed nerves. Not on your life! So the judge enjoyed the privilege through her office, which is not exactly what one would call ethical from a professional point of view.

At roughly the same time the Moscow authorities built a spacious new building for the Moscow Region Federal Arbitrage Court. True, there was one snag — according to the law, only the federal government is allowed to finance building works at the arbitrage court, in order to prevent the judges becoming dependent on the regional authorities. However, the website of the Moscow region Federal Arbitrage Court showed quite clearly that the city of Moscow was generous in its financing of the legal system, and was not hung up on formalities. In this case the formalities were the requirements of Article 124 of the Constitution, the Law on the Status of Judges and the Law on the Financing of the Courts, which categorically forbade any source of financing other than the federal budget. Forgive me for saying so, but if a judge admits that they consider the Constitution and other laws to be just formalities, then no further comment is required. What's more, another coincidence came to light — the people who built the court house and Maikova's apartment had one and the same surname. And this was not a case of strangers who just happened to share a common name. The father had been subcontracted to build the court house, and his son built an apartment for the judge.

* * *

So the new administrative resources, originally conceived as a counterbalance to the lawlessness of the oligarchs and widespread bribery, gradually began not just to eclipse the oligarchs' power, but to replace it. At some point, as is often the case, people in office began to think — 'my role is to implement the will of the state. But what if I perform this duty three times, and then the fourth time ask for a little something for myself? What's wrong with that? Nothing awful will happen, because I can judge what is right and wrong.'

From that moment the internal decay begins. 'I'm in office but I have to feed myself as well!' they would say. And it turns out that when you are in office you are always able to find some deals which need to be done. So if Putin's initial task was to purge the court system of oligarchical influence and crooked money, he then had to purge it of the influence of that part of the Presidential Administration which had decided that the courts were their personal business project and source of a decent income, and of the judges who had started to openly mess up their rulings.

When Medvedev took over as president, the long awaited changes began to happen. Dmitry Anatolevich (Medvedev), himself a lawyer and well acquainted with the practicalities of court work, began with a purge of the legal cadre, issuing a series of orders to appoint young and talented people whose task it was to challenge the status quo, and strictly limited the influence of the Presidential Administration on legal decisions. Several people who had worked in this area in the Presidential Administration lost their jobs, and the very structure of the court system was changed.

The arbitrage courts became more independent. Surprisingly, even after this decision many of the local authorities, in particular Moscow, continued to use all means at their disposal to reach an understanding with the courts. These smart guys would begin with primitive offers of cooperation, and could end up with direct attempts at bribery — and they were genuinely puzzled when they did not succeed.

Telephone law, under which the authorities could instruct the courts to take certain decisions, first began to operate in Russia a long time ago, long before the invention of the telephone even, but the changes which happened in the Kremlin administration meant that it now began to fail. It's worth pointing out that at this point Yuri Mikhailovich Luzhkov's faith in justice was fatally undermined. A man who had not lost a single court case in Moscow, notwithstanding how litigious he had been, suddenly suffered a painful defeat at the hands of Kremlin bogeyman Boris Nemtsov — and this was before Luzhkov had lost office. Unexpectedly, it became clear that the Federal authorities hated

Luzhkov even more than Nemtsov. And that was nothing to laugh about.

It was some time before Luzhkov was able to believe that a serious attack had begun against him. I remember the story which Boris Abramovich Berezovsky, who at that time was already living in London, told me. Looking back at his past life in Russia he told me that when the authorities threatened him, he laughed. But when they disconnected the electricity at his dacha, he knew things had got serious, and that it was time to run. I think that Yuri Mikhailovich recalled the wisdom of Berezovsky and realized that things were serious — that the authorities were tired of making hints and had given the command to attack — only when he had taken the post of dean of the Faculty for the Management of Large Cities in the International University in Moscow, and was asked if he genuinely planned to work for the symbolic salary of one ruble a month- following which the university was fined for violating the labor legislation. Of course one could understand why the Russian leadership acted as they did with Luzhkov.

The system can still fail, of course, especially in the regions, and it's clear that somewhere like the distant Cossack village of Kushchevskaya in Krasnodar region the courts will still pass judgments dictated to them by criminal gangs. They don't really have any choice — judges are mortals after all, and are subject to pressure and to murder attempts — sometimes they even end up dead. But now the authorities are doing a great deal to make the courts genuinely independent — raising the general material standards, equipping the court system properly, raising the salaries of judges and protecting their physical safety. So we really can talk about a fundamental change for the better. It's also important here to recognize the role of the court plenary meetings, which make recommendations which basically have a standing in law, and can be used in legal practice.

Be that as it may, the court system was probably the most important element in the retreat from the socialist system of state redistribution and the creation of the contemporary system of 'feeding'. Because it was the courts which could say to someone, for example, that as much as they wanted to get hold of a particular factory, it in fact belonged to Petr Petrovich Petrov, and it would be wrong to take it — that's no way to behave. Here also the officials managed to show that they were now in charge. Because when you have the entire financial might of the state behind you, your legal expenses become trifling, whereas a businessman has to pay up every time. So the very fact of being dragged into a court battle with state structures would always mean losses amounting to financial ruin for any company, while representing no threat at all to the state or the officials themselves.

If it has recently seemed that there is finally some hope of beating the system of 'feeding', then this is due in part to the improvements in the court system which we have observed. But just as there are no state structures which are divorced from society — they are in fact deeply embedded in society — it would be naive to think that it is possible to find the weakest link in order to break the whole chain. In this case, this formula of Lenin's unfortunately does not work. Here it is necessary to tackle several different problems on several fronts at the same time. And one of the main links in the chain which is strangling our country — strangling it through local exceptionalism and the system of 'feeding' — is the huge scale of the lies and falsehood which we see in the declarations of government spending and expenses.

CHAPTER 5

The city of Bryansk was engulfed in a wave of public protest. A mother and her daughter were run over at a pedestrian crossing which was marked with the proper sign, but the zebra on the asphalt was not visible because road works were under way. The three year old girl died at the scene. The woman who was driving the car had not attempted to flee the scene, and had even tried to administer some form of first aid, but it was no use — the child was already dead. Of course, rumours immediately began to circulate that the woman who had caused the accident would get off without any punishment, and it transpired that she already had four penalties for speeding, then someone said that she had relatives working in the prosecutor's office, or that she herself worked for the traffic police. Although, if she really worked there, it's unlikely she would have four cautions for speeding — usually they look after their own very well. But the public wasn't thinking about that. The public was enraged.

People came close to calling for a public lynching, they demanded that the woman be handed over, and were ready to rip her to pieces. There were rumors that she had posted some silly messages on some internet sites, which had increased the public's hatred. The story almost ended tragically, even though criminal proceedings had already begun two hours after the collision, and no one was trying to escape justice. And, to be honest, it was not entirely clear that the woman was responsible for the accident. The mother and her child had been crossing a pretty wide road — three lanes in one direction and three in the other — dodging the moving vehicles, walking round a bus to the right, rather than following the highway code, and the unfortunate woman, who will now live her whole life with the burden of having killed a child, did not even brake, because apparently she did not see, and had no hope of seeing, the mother and daughter in her path.

But the highway code clearly states that the driver is obliged to look ahead and if necessary take pre-emptive action. The highway code is right on that point. And we might say that this case has nothing to do with corruption. Where is the corruption? But then if you look closely enough, corruption's paw prints can be seen everywhere.

It turned out that a traffic police patrol vehicle, which filmed the incident, had been waiting not in front of the danger spot — there were frequently accidents at that pedestrian crossing — but behind it. Maybe that way it was easier to stop people and fine them. In fact, on one TV program a senior traffic policeman had said in their defense that the public expected them to fine people who broke the law. As awful as it might seem, he simply did not understand that the responsibility of the traffic police should be, in the first instance, to prevent violations and ensure safety on the roads. No one stopped to think how idiotic it was to encourage pedestrians to cross a road which was basically a motorway, with three lanes of traffic in both directions, by placing a zebra crossing on it. For some reason there is no rule that if a road has three lanes then a traffic light is needed, and if there is only one lane, then you can get by with a zebra crossing, but with a whole load of signs so that drivers can see it. And maybe it would makes sense for these kinds of crossings without lights on two or three lane highways to have sleeping policemen traffic calming bumps installed as well.

True, further investigations revealed that the Bryansk city administration knew about the problem, and no surprise that the decision had already been taken to pay for a traffic light at that danger spot. They even managed to work out how much a traffic light would cost there. It turned out to be one million rubles. But it seemed that there was no money in the local budget even for this purpose. The decision was taken, but of course not implemented — no money.

When I recounted this story on live TV, the phones really started ringing. One person who called was involved with selling traffic lights. He imported his goods from China, but installed them, strange as it may seem, in Italy. He was astonished by this price of one million rubles for one traffic light since according to his information the most popular model, even including the cost of importing it into Russia and getting it through customs, could never cost more than 87 thousand rubles. No way. And installing traffic lights is pretty easy these days — modern technologies enable you to avoid the hassle of connecting them to the electricity grid, there is equipment which uses an autonomous power source, works for several years and costs kopecks. What was the million rubles for? Where on earth did that kind of figure come from? Although it turns out that traffic lights costing an average of one to 1.2 million rubles are entirely commonplace in Russian towns. Apart from those towns where the local administration still has a shred of conscience. In those the whole caboodle somehow comes in at a little over one hundred thousand rubles.

This clearly gives us grounds to suspect that corruption is at play. As does the fact that the inhabitants of one Moscow district who wanted to put sleeping policemen on their street had to write a million letters and obtain a million approvals, and it will still end up costing 250,000 rubles. It's an interesting question, how exactly these sleeping policeman can cost so much money. Maybe a lavish funeral for a squad of real policemen has to be held on that spot? With full funeral rites on the 9th and 40th days, according to the Orthodox custom. I can't think of anything else. The person who naively bid for and won the tender in that city district said that the costs included endless absurdly large bribes to all the relevant departments above a certain size. Installing a sleeping policeman proved virtually impossible — unless of course you were the prosecutor, a member of the traffic police or someone from senior management. In that case it would take one phone call and the sleeping policemen would immediately find their way to the required spot, and no one need worry about how it gets done, or how much it costs. But if you're a ordinary member of the public, and you are unfortunate enough to have a school near your house, then have no doubts: getting the sleeping policemen installed will be a slow and painful process, and you won't get by without bribes.

So it turns out that corruption ended up costing the life of that three-year-old girl. But neither the mayor's office, the highways department, nor the people who designed the traffic system will answer for it. The driver will. It's always the underdog who is guilty. And the source of bribes remains, a fountain spouting eternal riches.

* * *

When you hear about how life in some town somewhere has suddenly become heaven on earth, and the mayor is no crook, you always ask — where's the catch? What kind of scam is going on? We know very well that it just can't be as simple as that. If a paving stone is being laid somewhere, we know that the mayor's wife is definitely involved somehow. If some plastic seating is being installed somewhere, then the factory which makes them must belong to the mayor's wife. There is no other possible explanation. True, all attempts to find out who the factories belong to which make the paving stones so ubiquitous in Monaco, and the relationship of the Prince of Monaco's wife to them, produced no worthwhile results. It seems that the inhabitants of that small but proud city state don't even think about these things. But we in Russia are used to assuming that our officials are always helping out their nearest and dearest. Often we are right, sometimes we are not.

Corruption at the very top attracts attention. Huge sums of stolen money, outlandish schemes, and massive embezzlement cases pleasantly tickle our imagination. Down at the everyday level we don't notice anything at all. But the consequences of this deep and deliberate degrading of the public morale are clear. When we get rid of one public official, we put another one in his place, and before too long the vampire inevitably bites again. Turn your back and a decent guy has again become a slave of the system.

When this system comes under attack, it begins to defend itself. When the system is described as corrupt, then everyone working in it promises to conduct a purge straight away. They claim not to be corrupt themselves, but admit that there are some individual rogue elements who need to be dealt with. 'We took those bribes because we didn't know it wasn't allowed!' they say. The impression we get is that everyone has completely lost their minds, and that the country is being run by Postman Pechkin from the children's cartoon. A huge army of Pechkin Postmen, at every level of government, are justifying their actions: 'Why was I so bad? Well, it was because I had no bike! But as soon as I get a bike, I will become a good person. Why did I steal? Well, it was because I didn't know that stealing was not allowed! As soon as I'm told that stealing is not allowed, I will become a good person.'

This was exactly the logic of Minister of Internal Affairs Rashid Gumarovich Nurgaliev, as we know. Why did the policemen, who at the time were still known as *militsiya*, get up to all sorts of dodgy business while they questioned people? It appears that it was because they didn't know that it's wrong to take bribes and torture people. So a document was produced to remind them clearly and plainly that a policeman should, surprise surprise, obey the laws of the Russian Federation. What a revolutionary concept! Many trainee policemen probably asked for their course fees back, as the whole point of the job had disappeared. But, to be honest, no one expects that policemen should be the brightest of people anyway. In the high-tech nuclear industry, the respected state body Rosatom has progressed much further.

Rosatom has put together some children's picture books which explain how corruption is a bad thing, and have written a brochure in wonderful bureaucratic language about how stealing really is quite damaging, how terrible corruption is and what problems it leads to. They put the publication of this wonderful work of literature out to tender, paid a king's ransom to the clever people behind it, and organized a whole series of courses, with the apparent aim of training their staff how to use this priceless instruction manual, and inculcating in them the steadfast conviction that they should never, for no reason, not in any circumstances, give in to the temptations of corruption.

It's pretty hard for me to imagine those important men, sitting at their classroom desks, exclaiming: 'Ah! So that's not allowed?! Come off it! What, that's also not allowed? No way! So that's supposed to be wrong is it?!' Turns out that the unfortunate Kant with his moral imperative had no idea what he was talking about. Turns out that we have managed to breed a whole race of people, who are completely lacking any moral imperative, they simply do not understand what is right and wrong. So just like in the Strugatskys' novel, they are cadavers whose basic needs are fully satisfied, who listen with interest to what is going on around them, devour everything which they can get their hands on, are quite content, but can't tell good from evil. They look like people, they move like people, but such finely calibrated concepts such as decency and honor, to say nothing of pangs of conscience and morality appear to be entirely missing. Someone forgot to load that program. Or maybe it was deleted somewhere along the way.

How touching. First off it makes you want to look your parents in the eye. If we have managed to breed officials which are an entirely new genetic type, then we could use them as a really terrible form of biological weapon! We should make efforts, using our contacts overseas, our agents Zatuliveter and Chapman, to introduce these genes among our enemies, and then we could quickly turn their countries into evil, corrupted places.

It's worth noting that the brochures and courses I mentioned (apparently the courses have become compulsory in some ministries, meaning that sizeable budgets are allocated to explaining to staff that stealing is in fact a sin) are entirely justified by the experiences of Russian history. The trusted worker and peasant cadres who were appointed as Soviet diplomats were taught etiquette in roughly the same way, so that no embarrassing situations arose during their work overseas due to the difference between village manners and those expected in diplomacy. They were taught in which hand to hold their knife and fork, how one should blow one's nose, if, heaven forbid, it should be necessary to do so, and why a serviette was better use than a curtain when your hands were dirty. So are we faced here with the same kind of situation? Do people really need to be told the difference between right and wrong? The state even spends money on it, and runs courses. Serious funds are allocated to it.

Although set against this background, there is actually a real fight being waged against corruption in Rosatom. True, it has a highly tenuous link to these courses — or in fact no link at all. This campaign was manifested in Sergey Vladilenovich Kirienko's personal refusal to cover for Rosatom's top bosses, or block investigations, or stop cases going to court. So as soon as these bosses found themselves in a situation where they were equal before the law, and the information was open, transparent and accessible, then things really got moving, and some of them even landed up in prison. Having seen their colleagues disappearing fast out of the neighboring offices, those that were left suddenly stopped using the excuse that no one had told them what they shouldn't do, and stopped thieving.

Kaluga region became famous for using similar methods to tackle corruption — I don't mean those stupid brochures and strange courses. Ten years ago Kaluga region was famous for its miserable roads and horrible dilapidated buildings, left behind by the state project to build a center for science which would have become Russia's Silicon Valley. At the same time everyone knew the sad truth that the state didn't have enough money, and that the foundations of the buildings would stand for eternity, until they were destroyed by some catastrophe or simply obscured by the sands of time. But then Anatoly Dmitrievich Artamonov became governor, and in the space of ten years Kaluga region shot ahead from its initial position of 80th amongst Russia's regions. In recent years, Kaluga region has been in third place according to average income, trailing only Moscow city and Moscow region, and having previously been a region which was dependent on the federal budget, it will soon become a net contributor.

And this is a region without oil, gas or other natural resources — although there was an electricity supply and there was land. So what did Artamonov do? He recognized that this was a region where factories had operated in the Soviet period. Now it had a center for scientific research, Obninsk, with a functioning atomic power station. It had places of historical interest — Maloyaroslavets, where the battle took place which forced Napoleon to retreat along the New Smolensk road rather than the Old Smolensk road. It had a God- fearing people, sacred places, monasteries, hermitages. Artamonov told the people of Kaluga region they could do anything they wanted to!

Artamonov himself was no outsider — he was a local man, from the countryside. He was schooled in Soviet administrative, economic and party work. Hard to say much about his political views — more accurate to describe him as a good manager, which is probably a good thing as far as regional governors are concerned. Artamonov decided that he wanted to attract some car building giants to set up in the region. And unexpectedly, he succeeded. So how exactly did he tempt them? With a bribe? Not the directors and shareholders of Volkswagen and Volvo!

Or somehow do a shady deal with Samsung? Not likely. This kind of persuasion wouldn't work — in this case he had to do things differently.

Artamonov proposed a scheme which, if unsuccessful, could have ended with criminal proceedings, not just his dismissal from office. He decided that the regional government would use its own money to make the factory grounds ready. It would supply the land, and pay for linking it up to the heating, water and electricity supplies, and all the other necessary connections. He just asked the firms to come there, build their factories, and take the people of Kaluga to work in them. If they needed they could build a town to house their specialists. If they needed highly qualified engineers, technical and operational staff, then in Kaluga they had the only branch of the Bauman University outside Moscow, and they would open a department in it especially for the companies to train the people they needed.

And so Volkswagen played ball, favoring Kaluga over Nizhny Novgorod or Leningrad regions. Refusing to rest on his laurels, Artamonov decided to open a special industrial zone. If foreign investors come in the beginning, then with time, Russian ones, even the most conservative, would see that no one is being conned here, that western companies are working effectively, and will also join in. I asked Artamonov if his staff weren't creating obstructions. He explained that every investor had his personal mobile phone number. At any moment of day or night they could call with any question. He pointed out that we'd been talking for several hours and the telephone hadn't rung once. Because there weren't any problems. No reason to phone. The people who worked for Artamonov knew why they were doing this. The investors must be able to work without any problems. Because Artamonov's aim was for the region's inhabitants to have high salaries and a decent standard of living.

Of course one shouldn't get too carried away about this example — salaries in Kaluga region are still not the same as in Germany. And of course there are still a million negative aspects, like the increasing price of fossil fuels, which push all the other price upwards. But the region really has come to life! Fundamental changes have taken place. Work has appeared. People began to ask where they can live, and Artamonov's response was that the state, in the form of the regional government would let people rent the land they needed, and if a family has more than one child, it's free, and the regional government will connect up the homes with roads, electricity and gas. So the price of a square meter of property fell sharply. In Kaluga itself, on the right bank of the Oka river, a large new accommodation district called Pravgorod has been erected. For those specialists who were invited to come and work accommodation was built which could be rented cheaply — a higher quality form of what we would call hostel accommodation — come and live here was the message. And so it appears that with the necessary will these kinds of problems can be solved. And in no time the roads were improved, more young people began to stay in Kaluga rather than move to Moscow and Moscow region — because a real boss had appeared in the region.

When I asked Artamonov whether there was corruption in his region, he answered that it was actually very easy to tackle corruption. He took no bribes, which means that no one in his team took bribes. Any sign of bribe taking would be treated as a criminal offence. No one would be sheltered. And that's the right approach. Artamonov understands very well that it is essential to train a new type of government official.

In the preceding chapter we looked in detail at the failings of Russia's court system. It's hard to say what more President Medvedev could have done for Russia's judges. The court buildings are impressive, their salaries are large, and they are protected by the law in every way possible. But the problem is the quality of the staff in the court system. What kind of person works as a judge in Russia? A very large number of them are former court secretaries — girls who started work at the age of 17-18 and from that time on came to see other people only in the role of plaintiff. Another large category are former members of the law enforcement structures who are also used to seeing other people either as criminals or victims. Our concept of a judge is that he should be not only a specialist in the law, but also a genuinely wise person — whether we like it or not he determines our fate. People have a tendency to yearn for ideals. But where have we actually seen judges like this? In the cinema, and in western novels. Russian reality is normally quite different.

In order to avoid repeating the mistakes made in the court system, when officials are divorced from real life from an early age and then continue their professional development inside a bureaucratic structure, with no understanding of what really makes the country tick, Artamonov forced the staff of his administration who had reached a certain level in their career such as deputy minister, to go off and govern the region from the 'shop floor'. To manage a real business, working until you are tired enough to drop, and you know you can't go on, but you just have to. And then you see your colleagues' work in a completely different light. Then you look at them not from the neighboring office, but from the other end of the career ladder. And then the value of experience, the value of real human relations, and the cost of a mistake, become clear. Then, after several years, when the official returns to the position of minister, he has a much better understanding of real life.

The result is a wonderful staff training system, which combines a range of different experiences. The official understands how the system really works, and doesn't simply sign documents mindlessly. And in this way a class of professional managers is produced who are not simply personally devoted to the governor, but are devoted to the idea of effective work and service — after all, they are familiar with the needs of the people 'on the ground', having lived with them side by side for several years and heard what they have to say. And, of course, as professionals they need to constantly improve their qualifications, so it is compulsory for them to travel abroad on training courses twice a year. And if there are other Russian regions where something positive and interesting is happening, they travel there to learn from their experience. Or if it's happening in Singapore, America, France, Italy or Germany, then they go there. But not just to go on a shopping spree — to actually study.

Corruption always happens for a reason in Russia. It always spreads from the top down and from the bottom up at the same time. The famous saying about how a fish rots from the head down is actually a long way from the truth. If our fish begins to rot, then it rots all over. It's just that if no example of honesty is being set right at the top, then all the lower levels know what they can get away with, and they copy it — only on a different scale, since they don't have quite the same range of options for doing favors for friends and family.

CHAPTER 6

In Russia the popular perception is that the fight against corruption takes two main forms. The first is the removal from office of upstart political opponents who have gotten so out of control that they have started to take more than they are entitled to and are forgetting to share it with their bosses. So everyone understands that this person has ceased to be part of the system, a team player, a member of the collective, but has become an irritant, who has to be gotten rid of. The second reason for talking about the fight against corruption is when an official may have behaved well, but there has been a change of management, a new team has arrived which wants to place its own trusted people in charge of the money flows and redirect them from one group which has got used to 'feeding' to another, hungry group, which has arrived and is impatiently waiting its turn.

I know that many of you will cry out joyfully that you know who I am talking about. But I'm afraid I have to disappoint you. What I'm talking about here is a tradition which has been going on for at least a thousand years. Because the practice of directing financial channels in favor of your own people could be witnessed in the court of any Russian tsar, since a lobby group appears around any leader which makes the procurement decisions and steals property, and so people who embezzle on a fantastic scale go down in the pages of history.

There was most probably never a period in history when it was possible to say with confidence exactly how much it really costs to lay a road, or to build some building. The system characterized by a corrupt elite and bribery, for which our own period appears to be so famed, has actually existed since the dawn of time. It is, I stress, a national tradition. It's laughable that we don't even need to think up any new schemes. Just re-read Saltykov-Shchedrin and it's exactly like today! And that's just for starters. Why is it essential to study *Dead Souls* in school? Many people naively assume that it is just an encyclopedia detailing that period in history. Nothing of the sort! It's the most accurate business handbook explaining the Russian national mentality. In fact to this day dead souls still roam different accounting systems, and unexpectedly appear and then disappear after elections. State welfare provision works exactly in that way, making good use of this concept of dead souls.

At one moment it appeared that victory against corruption was already in the bag. We just needed to sign some documents from Europe, learn from foreign experience, and suddenly everything would be fine. All our officials would declare their incomes honestly, and the public would happily believe them. If we want we can even make family members accountable! Of course they will dig in their heels for a while, as was the case when the president introduced this initiative, and they will make a fuss that it's dangerous, various orders will be issued which will excuse even the closest family members from completing income declarations, but then under pressure from the Kremlin this accountability problem will be resolved.

That is in fact how it happened. But one small clause, a tiny amendment, remained unsigned, thus turning everything described above into empty words. When the clock struck midnight, all the legal initiatives turned into a pumpkin and we still had no golden carriage in which to ride into the bright future. The purpose of the amendment was to oblige officials to declare not just incomes but — far more importantly — outgoings, and to give an additional declaration if the second sum exceeded the first, since it's clear that if the difference was over a certain amount, then there was a real problem which needed to be dealt with.

* * *

If you ask officials at any level why they wanted to work where they do, it turns out that every single one of them was motivated only by the public interest. Of course we have no reason to doubt that. Representatives of political parties one and all are also consumed by public interest, and during their speeches say identical things with almost identical words, and their programs are virtually identical too. It's good that they write who is from which party on their T-shirts, otherwise it would be hard to tell. And they are all bursting with concern for the people. They want the very best for us all. And I'm almost ready to believe it. Although one seditious thought comes to mind: maybe it's not enough to want. Maybe you need to know how to deliver as well?

Take this example. I have absolutely no idea how to conduct an orchestra, none whatsoever. My mother didn't send me to music school, for which I am very grateful. I can't read music at all. But I know who to call, and who I need to strike a deal with, in order to become the conductor of almost any orchestra. What stops me is that I of course don't know how to conduct. But I am completely sure that will in no way hinder those people who will sign the documents appointing me. In fact I'm a pretty decent chap. I'm easy to get on with. I understand how the world works. I know who are my friends and who are my enemies. I know when to show compassion towards the fallen, and which of them will rise again. People like me are usually called wise, clever, refined, knowledgeable, well-connected. And taking all that into account does the small detail that I don't know how to conduct really matter? When do such details matter in the modern world? We might assume that among those people who act like they are in charge of us, someone at least knows what they are doing. Surely you have to know something, and have some talent, to become a minister, a member of parliament, or member of the Federation Council?

In 1996 I was driving along listening to the Silver Rain radio station — then the station had just opened and I had not yet started working there — and I thought how great it was that there were no politicians on this radio station. Because whenever I happened to switch over to some other radio station, some person or another was making a speech. And every time I found myself wondering why exactly that person had gone into politics. Sure, you could just about understand it back in the Soviet period: they took a guy by the scruff of the neck, dragged him through the necessary bureaucratic procedures, cut him to shape, dressed him up. And then he stood on the mausoleum, in his pork pie hat and his little grey coat, his cheeks puffed up. And another ten exactly like him stood by his side — and they were all identical, just like hamsters, standing rooted to the ground, watching. And it's somehow obvious that they hate each other, but can't do anything about it. And you think to yourself that they must be failures. If they had been successful, they would be diplomats somewhere. They would get big color televisions and video players and cars through their contacts. Then they would be surrounded by beautiful things and their lives would be sweet. Instead they are standing on the mausoleum in identical overcoats, cold and bored. But no one forced our modern-day politicians to get up onto the mausoleum, so why did they decide to go into government?

In reality politicians need to have some sort of overarching goal, some sort of logical system to describe their actions. I'm ready to understand Boris Gryzlov's motivation — if he wasn't in politics he wouldn't have been able to play football. I recognize, but do not share, Andrey Fursenko's goal — he was probably waiting his whole life for someone to propose that the Russian word for coffee should become neuter rather than masculine. But what drove the others? Imagine the reaction of Mrs Golikova when she was summoned and told that she would become

Health Minister. If you ask me her answer should have been: 'You must be joking. Me? Minister of Health? I'm a financier, all this medicine, patients, grannies — it's not my thing.' But the terrible thing is that the respected Tatyana Alekseevna (Golikova) did not utter these words, but saluted her seniors, and went off to work in medicine, knowing absolutely nothing about it. I imagine that the first present she was given when she started her work was a white doctor's coat, and then a short handbook to being a doctor. But surely that is not enough. Because it's not possible to manage medicine from the perspective of a financier. Profit, loss — that's not hard to understand. But the only thing is that in medicine profit means the maternity ward, loss is the morgue, and the real problem is what happens between them.

What's more the recent tendency is to appoint people from business to government management positions. But they take these people to manage those sectors in which their businesses operated. Of course there is no way at all that they are going to help out their former companies! We can be quite sure of that! It just kind of happens by itself, completely naturally. And we, naturally, accept it. For example, can we imagine that the Minister for Agriculture, Mrs Skrynnik abandons all her businesses, which operated in that same field, and deliberately begins to do all she can to destroy her own company, which was one of the best? Of course not. It was precisely because of her successful business that Elena Borisovna (Skrynnik) gained her reputation as a manager and was asked to work in the government.

Or can you imagine that at the same time as Mr Kostikov managed the securities market his company AVK, through which he came up as a specialist, ended up being really unsuccessful. It would never happen. True, when Igor Vladimirovich (Kostikov) lost his position, his company also quickly disappeared from the market.

No one should have any illusions here. But what is even more interesting is that none of this is really seen as corruption, but as the natural order of things. So when the former head of the Southern district of Moscow was accused over his son's involvement in the finances of the utilities and communal services in that district, he had no idea what was wrong. So the wife of the mayor of Moscow is allowed to operate in the building industry, but the son of the district head is not allowed to work in communal services? Why not?

Almost every minister has affiliated companies or friends in the relevant branches of industry, and they are quite comfortable in the knowledge that he trusts them and understands that only they can do what is needed, while others for some reason cannot. After all, was it not possible to conduct a competition once which resulted in Berezovsky and Abramovich's team getting Sibneft, when the competition commission was headed by their partner in crime, Mr Patarkatsishvili? It sure was. Did it bother anyone? No, it didn't. The law was not yet drafted, no codex had been written. What about the salaries? What's the difference what the salaries are? The people work effectively, and understand what needs to be done for their branch of industry to grow. And when they begin, quite naturally, to lobby the interests of their own companies, of course that's not corruption — what do you mean?! It's just them being professional. When the boss of a major car building firm, who earns several thousand dollars a month (I hate to think what that salary would look like in rubles!), suddenly gets a middle-ranking position in the ministry which happens to deal with car building, it's quiet clear to me that far from being the ultimate example of lobbying, this is just a case of man wanting to serve his country! This is quite easy for me to understand — although to do so I need to switch off 99% of my brain.

But we should not forget that in such situations, according to current legislation the relevant company should be handed over to be temporarily managed as a trust. Our Duma deputies set a shining example — of course their last reason for entering the Duma is to protect the interests of their businesses! True, certain questions arise: what about the scandalous case of Duma deputy Mr Egiazaryan, when a certain state official apparently handed him a suitcase full of money, which the Duma deputy then used to embark on some sort of ill-fated deal? Or was that some kind of bad joke? Whenever you open the newspaper and read how Duma deputies and members of the Federation Council talk with no shame about their businesses, then you feel quite embarrassed, especially if you have up until now held the naive view that the laws which they pass could in any way threaten the business which feeds them. After all, they are Duma deputies, not idiots. They may be guilty of many things, but idiocy is not one of them.

What's more, if we take a compassionate view, who is going to argue that they are not behaving completely appropriately. After all, they do real work, and even don't take any money from the state for it, not ever. It's just that after a certain period of time they will get, in one form or another, the profit from the growth of the company which they own.

What is happening here is a mutual delegation of powers. And the examples of the Duma deputies or members of the Federation Council who bombard every single existing or non-existent government office with deputies' questions, show not only that they are trying to make back the money which they had to pay for their seats, but their sincere desire to support the businesses which they continue to run. I have observed many times on my TV show, for example, how Vladimir Volfovich Zhirinovsky angrily cursed the governor of Krasnodar Region Aleksandr Nikolaevich Tkachev, and it soon became clear why he was angry — it turned out that at some point certain wishes of Vladimir Volfovich's were not taken into account, when they really should have been.

Lobbying, yes indeed. Yes, a convoluted system of personal connections. But how could it be any other way? At the start of this book we examined how someone becomes a quiet and humble hospital worker. And we established that he can't live on the money he earns, so he has to find some other way of getting by. So he will accept a bit of gratitude from the patients — not just in the form of warm words, let's put it like that. He himself doesn't even ask for any money. The patients decided themselves to give it. No one is to blame here, that's just how it turned out. They bring their money, express their gratitude, and that is how it is at every level of society, and the longer it goes on the more our lives begin to look like that fictional square in the fictional Central Asian town — with a table, chair, red telephone, and people waiting in line to give money. Not because it is compulsory, but because that is the accepted way, the natural order of things, and it just makes our lives easier to live.

* * *

So let's continue. Imagine the most terrible situation: your close acquaintance becomes a boss somewhere. You go to see him and tell him that since he has just become a manager, and believe it or not, but you have a company working in the very same business, maybe he could help you out by placing an order with your company? And if he were to reply no, what would you say about him? Of course you wouldn't believe it. You'd think he has gone crazy. What difference is it to him who he helps? You've worked together for so many years, it's completely normal to expect him to help! You assure him that he can trust you to do everything just right.

And it works exactly the same way in reverse. For example, let's take any one of you readers, and appoint you to a government position. You sit down and begin to think OK, you're going to be honest, you'll organize the work, and find out what's going on in this area of industry. So who can tell you about that? Oh yeah, you know some great guys, who are doing business in exactly that area, they're talented, sensible guys, you'll get them over! And so you get them over, you talk at length with them, discussing all the finer details and nuances, and they assure you that everything will be just fine. Why doesn't your wife go and work for them. It really would be better for her to work there, the salary is better, and the conditions are incomparable. And your son is growing up, just finished at the institute, still a pretty dim lad, how can you get him set up? And so your new acquaintances suggest that they get him a job in their partner company, where he can grow into a man. Wonderful, just great.

Of course, it is wonderful. And everything becomes clearer and clearer. You are so sure that everyone around you is thieving, that you invest your money completely honestly in tenders, and organizations which you trust, in other words, with those same new acquaintances. And it's not important that their company was registered yesterday or the day before yesterday — you know the people behind it and you are totally sure that they would never steal anything. So you really try to do everything possible so that their company gets that order. Because in the last resort, if you want you can phone up the director and remind him that you did a deal, the way it's done in Russia. And no bribes changed hands at all. Although a Mercedes then turns up from nowhere. Or someone gives you that typical Russian winner's prize — a Swiss watch. No one will say how much they cost — although it's not right to give someone at that level some second-rate watch. And the further you rise in office, the more gifts you get. No one is extorting any money, don't you worry! Just everyone knows how to get on with each other. And favor follows favor, and before you know it, their company has a monopoly on the market. And you're not doing too badly either. But then suddenly you get removed from office, and of course the company disappears in a shot as well!

But what does this case tell us about the pervasiveness of corruption and thieving in Russia? Who is thieving? Everyone is just working, they're just earning a living. OK, the companies are front companies. But that is just to prevent people from stealing! Just to be sure that no one can do a runner, and that everyone is doing their jobs. You know everyone involved, they are all respectable people. It goes on at all levels, just that when it happens at a higher level, then different sums of money are involved. But you know who we are working with — they are top rate, decent people. And they really are. They'll come along and tell you that you'll never believe it but everyone is thieving! And you're shocked, and you tell them that it mustn't be allowed. We must use all means at our disposal to fight theft. What is theft, after all? Theft is when money leaves the family. And when it is spent unwisely within the family — what can you do, no one is perfect.

* * *

If we're discussing the traditional means of fighting bribery and embezzlement of public funds in Russia, it's impossible to avoid looking at the corruption scandals which took place during the reign of Peter I, when everyone was thieving like mad. So who was the most corrupt of them all? Aleksandr Danilovich Menshikov, an ally of the Tsar, an outstanding statesman, and a man known for his unbounded self-interest. How was he able to get away with so much? Well it's no great mystery. He would fall at his highness's feet, show his remorse, do a funny turn, make him laugh, and everything would be just fine. Corruption was rife under Catherine II as well. Who was corrupt? The court favorites of course! Why was his Highness Prince Tavrichesky not beheaded, why did he not end up in prison or even lose his place at court for his Potemkin Village con trick? Did he really manage to deceive the Empress? No, Ekaterina was a wise ruler and knew very well that it was a blatant con, but Potemkin could get away with things that no one else could. Why did the corruption suddenly disappear when Pavel came to power? Because he had no friends. He didn't know how to make friends, and didn't want to anyway. True, this meant that he was unable to stand up to the so-called English conspiracy, which lead to him being physically removed by a group of officers.

There is of course a widespread belief that foreign countries have simple and transparent government systems where corruption is impossible. These are countries which are generally described as democracies. But this belief is wrong, because when you look closer, you find that it's impossible to make these kinds of generalizations. There may well be a low level of corruption in some democracies, but it cannot be ruled out that this social ill will flourish at some point. Countries like China and India demonstrate that at different periods in their history there may be more or less corruption. The death penalty is undoubtedly a restraining factor, but you have to understand that in order to implement the death penalty for embezzlement of state funds, you first need to get the permission of the party bosses to sacrifice one or another of their members who has been caught thieving.

It's clear that in Russia the power structures were always pretty corrupt, but the essence of this corruption was different from what we have today. In our times corruption normally means illegal personal enrichment, but in Russia it was always the state which was doing the corrupting, and whole social groups, even classes were corrupted. If you think about it, under the Soviet system of state redistribution, some workers got better rations due to their class allegiance, and district Communist Party committee secretaries enjoyed the privilege of stocking up in the closed sections of the department stores. While this may not have been corruption exactly, it was a social order which was certainly a long way from fair, in which it was impossible for people to ever be fully equal before the law, and your standard of living depended not so much on your financial means as on your position in the hierarchy. And this continues to this day. The traditional Russian disapproval of taking ' above your station' applies to this day, and those who have taken more than their rank or grade entitles them to are put to shame for it. Although in general everyone is allowed to take what they can. If we want to create a society where no one can take anything, regardless of their rank or grade, we first need to clearly determine the nature of this power structure, and the various entitlements allocated to different levels in it.

In the army, an eternal triangle exists, based on age, rank and position. But state officials are ruled by an additional fourth criterion, which allows you to rise quickly, if not according to age, then by rank and position: who you are friends with. Who are you doing a favor for? Who will always look after your interests and bring you exactly what you need? When Vladimir Ilich Lenin was arguing against the opinion, held in the Communist Party, that private ownership of land should be allowed, he wrote a letter to Bukharin, if I remember rightly, in which he said that 'private ownership of land leads inevitably to the development of capitalism'. The existing wildly unfair system of pay for state sector workers, from the women working in the social welfare service, to the traffic police, leads in the same way to the spread of corruption at all levels, as we know very well.

So the general view in society is that if you are a traffic policeman at a certain grade, then we are willing to give you a certain amount of money for a traffic violation. But if you ask for more than you are entitled to, we will make a fuss that it's terrible, that you are all corrupt rogues, scoundrels and scum, and you all need to be executed. If you are a school teacher, then of course we understand that your salary is small, so we will top it up by a certain amount. If you are a nurse, then we will bring you a box of chocolates at the hospital. And if you are doctor, then we won't stop at flowers and bottles of perfume, there will be envelopes full of money as well. I remember an old story from the 1970s, when Andrey Makarevich was stopped for speeding by the traffic police. Andrey Vadimovich (Makarevich) sheepishly tried to interest the policeman in a recording by his group Mashina Vremeni, to which he got the reply that it would be best for him to just give the policeman some money, then he could buy that record, and Andrey's friends' records too.

This brazenness — 'just give me the money' — has penetrated all levels of society. But this is mainly because the idea of a state sector employee living honestly, whether he is a minister or anyone else, is seen as a joke in this country. This explains the wealth of ministers' wives, who are often in effect the managers or the beneficiaries of all those businesses where their husbands worked tirelessly before getting into government, and the widespread phenomenon of ministers' 'friends', whose friendliness often knows no bounds. Often they just turn up and begin negotiating with the companies which work in a given sphere, explaining that they may not themselves be the minister, but they are the minister's right hand man. And although previously this meant 'deputy minister', now these words have taken on much more significance. Now the minister's right hand man is, as a rule, the person who answers for the minister's private finances, and he really does have the power to tackle any issue. Because recently ministers at the federal and regional levels — and in fact not only them but anyone who works in government — have become cleverer, so they won't be silly enough to take a bribe themselves. These days you can't just take them cash in an envelope. Instead payment will be in the form of a credit transfer by some convoluted route, or a payment to an affiliated company, which will be only too happy to present you with a bill and will help you out with something you need doing. But who owns that company? The minister's friends and former classmates do. Of course, we believe that they win all the tenders by fair competition alone! Just that the terms of the competition and tenders are a little bit skewed.

The tender put out by the company Teledyne Industries International, operating in Russia, comes to mind. When Mr Yakubovsky, who headed the Russian branch of the firm, was in a car accident which he miraculously survived, he was jokingly told that he could buy any car, as long as it had two 'W's in its name. That is basically how tenders are organized in Russia, for example for the car used by the ambulance service — as a rule the terms of such competitions are spelled out pretty clearly.

* * *

In order to identify all these imperfections, all the ugliness which would come to the surface if everyone in Russia tried to live honestly for three months (on the fourth month it would prove impossible, since anyone in any government position would resign, unable to survive on their official salaries), we need the equivalent of that drop of magic 'Fairy' washing-up liquid which breaks up the grease on the dirty plate quickly and effectively. Such a method exists, and it is very simple. It involves bringing people into government who are not friends of the boss, but educated and capable specialists, chosen on the basis of their professional qualities. This means that there should be a career structure which is open to everyone in the country, a system for professional promotion, known sometimes as the 'social elevator'. If this social elevator currently works along the lines of 'show me how to love you, I will love you passionately, and in return I will get wherever I want', it needs to be replaced with 'show me what you have achieved, and I will assess your professional capabilities and send you off for further training, and when you are ready you will get a position in government.'

This is pretty much what Artamonov in Kaluga region is doing. And it's no coincidence that in medieval China there was for many centuries an effective system for finding state officials, based solely on their talent, so a well-educated young man, even from the deepest provinces, could get a senior appointment because he had passed the state exam with top marks. How can we talk about passing a state exam with top marks if our notorious Unified State Exam is already the object of ridicule across the internet, just like the order personally signed by Minister for Education and Research Mr Fursenko which contained three spelling mistakes, and the brilliant speech delivered in English by the minister for Sport, Tourism and Youth Politics which was met with nothing but tears of laughter. Although it's quite possible to believe that there were no grammatical mistakes in the speech, because it was written for him, rumor has it on good grounds that the English words were written with Russian letters — since the minister for Sport and Tourism, notwithstanding his doctorate level education, got a mark for the accompanying basic level language exam which was embarrassingly low. It would have been better if he had just said honestly that he speaks menu-level English, although the menu in question would probably be for McDonald's.

The most effective and simple method for fighting corruption would involve not only stopping lying to ourselves, but also recognizing that friends are the people we drink tea with and occasionally meet at a restaurant. The typical criticism directed at Vladimir Putin, that his friends head the biggest holding companies, and many of them are also ministers in the government, tend to be true. Indeed, if we consider who has become hugely rich in the last eight years, and how, then we could of course acknowledge their fantastic entrepreneurial talents, although everyone knows that following a change of regime these people would very likely repeat the fate of the talented entrepreneur Baturina, whose continued success was based on the simple fact that her husband Yuri Mikhailovich Luzhkov occupied the position of mayor of Moscow.

When it comes to how talented and clever Russia's entrepreneurs are, we should point out that not a single one of them can boast of success in taking their business model to the West, or of managing to make a profit in that business environment even closely comparable to the money they made in Russia. Here I have in mind not entrepreneurs of the scale of Evgeny Kaspersky, who it would be hard to accuse of having any friends, but those oligarchs whose success was based solely on their ability to make friends.

Here the first amongst equals is the great phlegmatic Roman Arkadevich Abramovich, who displayed no business acumen beyond this ability to make friends. But this ability did him a lot of favors, and demonstrated yet again that silence is golden. His court case against Boris Abramovich Berezovsky, which has now entered the final phase, has shown that careless talk costs money, and that holding your tongue, and being on good terms with people, is the best route to riches. Although one should say that in this case we are witnessing something which is rare in

Russia, when both sides are as bad as each other: one can't say that one of them is a Chatsky and the other a Molchalin from Griboedov's comedy. Probably both of them are as unpleasant as Molchalin, and if Abramovich is a Molchalin without any marriage plans, then Berezovsky is a Molchalin wannabe: he's got a bad attitude, and he continues wriggling like a little devil and spouting complete nonsense.

A vivid example of Berezovsky's inability to adapt to new circumstances is the fact that after so many years living in England he has still not been able to learn the language to any decent level. This doesn't indicate a lack of talent — he is without doubt a gifted man — just an amazing contempt for the country he is in and the people he lives with, and a sincere conviction that nothing else in the world is of any importance other that he himself. Although I think that life has shown Boris Abramovich how wrong he is.

* * *

But what then is corruption for us in Russia? Is it something alien to us or not? It's very clear that we have always had corruption, that it is still with us and will be with us in the future. But what is amazing is this tendency to demand that the government should somehow be different from us. The people who govern us at all levels should be more advanced, more honest, more forward-thinking than the population as a whole. But as we have already discussed, for the majority of us a refusal to help coming from a former classmate, or neighbor who has got ahead is, to put it mildly, hard for us to understand. It conflicts with our concept of right and wrong. We have come to see this kind of helping hand not as corruption but rather as a clan instinct, a gut feeling that these are 'our guys' who we can work with. It's always been like that in Russia.

In those countries where democracy means the equality of all before the law, the main outcome is that the private property owned by the king and the private property of the poorest of citizens is equally important in the eyes of the law, and needs to be protected in the same way. In Russia this is just empty words, it means absolutely nothing. Here people can become wealthy or destitute based entirely on the politics of the moment, not as the result of a fair legal decision.

What has this got to do with the fight against corruption? A lot, in fact. Because we can only purge ourselves of the evils of corruption when the public as a whole, not just the authorities, recognize that it is unacceptable. But the Russian people cannot see that corruption is unacceptable, because a strong clan instinct has lived in the collective conscience from ancient times. We have never recognized all citizens as having equal rights. That sort of nonsense would never enter our minds. Pretty much the only formal principle of democracy which we have accepted is the principle that every person has a single vote. But no Russian has ever thought that democracy should mean the creation of a political and legislative system which protects private property, because the concept of private property is not sacred to us, and never will be. There has not been a single generation which has been able to live their lives in the homes of their fathers and forefathers without the constant threat that it could be taken from them or that something else bad would happen. And because of this corruption is seen as part of a collective social guarantee, and the clan mentality as a form of defense against outside forces.

When this kind of system operates, the clan which comes to power begins to steal like crazy. If we look into the recent past, this kind of theft was restrained by various inspection processes from the top down and bottom up, by the Party control committee and other organs, and by the fact that it wasn't anyway so necessary. Once you had come to power and sat at the highest level of the social hierarchy, your personal wellbeing grew to such an extent that you had no need to struggle to feed yourself or to achieve a higher standard of living. The very fact that you were at the top gave you everything you needed. But today the fact of being in power only allows you to join the system. That is in itself is worth a lot, of course, but you still have to work to get that fabled 'everything'. No one is going to just give you a government dacha, and in any case you wouldn't particularly want one, because these days those government dachas are worse than those giant town houses which the rich inhabitants of the Rublyevka neighborhood build themselves. So your sense of the standards you need to aspire to also changes.

These days we have realized that inequality, including material equality, can be found everywhere, in many different forms. How pleasing it is when you are sitting somewhere with company, and suddenly the wistful melody of the *Vertu* telephone comes from your pocket, indicating that yet another person has stumped up a crazy sum of money for a fancy item of jewelry, a kind of eulogy for money senselessly spent. No surprise that the *Vertu* is so popular amongst the corrupt generals — some of whom walk around with several of them in their pockets. But as is usual in Russia, their excuse is that the phone is allegedly a fake, or that it was given to them as a present by their friends at the factory. And no one stops to think that buying fake phones is unacceptable, or that they shouldn't really be accepting these kinds of presents.

Russian officialdom's love for yachts, foreign property and incredibly expensive watches, in other words their blatant vulgarity, is already notorious. Vladimir Resin will deservedly go down in history not as the person who restored the Bolshoi Theatre, but as the owner of a million euro watch, and for his incredibly stupid attempt to justify having it — that they apparently cost not a million but much less, 30 thousand euros. He will never live that down. But is he the only one? How many governors and ministers have become famous for their whole-hearted, inappropriate infatuation with expensive playthings? How does this impact on peoples' trust in government? We know very well that those people who appear on our TV screens could never have got all those things honestly. Granted, some of them may have been in business at some point, but they are now adorned with so many different trinkets, and you know that their whole year's salary wouldn't be enough to buy a single one of them.

* * *

As paradoxical as it might sound, Russian corruption is linked to our slave mentality, to the fact that reputation means nothing in our country. Public opinion has no impact at all on the careers of public officials. Over the course of centuries all aspects of Russians' lives were governed by whether the Tsar was happy. The terrible truth was that success or failure in one's career depended first and foremost on the favorable attitude of the powers that be, and only then on ability, talent, knowledge and skills. It was little wonder that such a large number of great men ended their days in exile or in disfavor — and a similar fate could befall both Petr Yakovlevich Chaadaev and Aleksandr Vasilevich Suvorov. If we observe that at no single point in Russian history was it possible to rely on a fair trial or honest laws, or on the real equality of all, then it is clear that to this day our wellbeing and our success depend on the clan which we belong to.

And we are not going to change. Everything which we despise in the ethnic minority populations, which spread and corrupt everything around them, placing their own people in the right places, all this we find disgusting because it is a gross satirical reflection of how all Russians live. Only that our clans are often based not on ethnic or religious identity, but on the principle of who you know and your relationship with important people. So we may see the ethnic minorities as a reflection of our national identity and reject them with loathing, but we still forgive ourselves. Again, we don't want to recognize our own infallibility, just as we don't want to understand that the solution lies not in beating our heads against the floor of the church, mosque or synagogue, but in the clear and simple recognition of the equality of all before the law, and respect for professionals.

But we are in no hurry to give up personal devotion in favor of professionalism.

Of course there are much simpler psychological and technical means of fighting corruption. They are well known — in particular passing all the articles, without exception, of the Convention against Corruption, including strict control to ensure that the expenses of officials and their families are justified. But all of this is secondary, since any attempt to reshape human nature needs more than just laws. Often we see the reverse happening — if the laws are imported from abroad, and are not a product of the long-suffering experience of the Russian people, their implementation is subverted by the people and their problems.

One terrible example is what happened several decades after those black Americans decided on a wave of nostalgia to return to Africa and create the independent democratic state of Liberia. There is no need to describe the living nightmares which ensued there, as the 20th Century closed. It's no coincidence that all the countries of Asia or Africa which have enjoyed some level of success have never been complete democracies — they have always had some major non-democratic features. If we examine this properly, it's clear that what we might call model democracy only exists in countries where the majority of the population has a particular kind of mind-set.

I don't want to get into the finer details of the link between national mentality and the form of government in a country, but it is pretty hard to find a Muslim country which is democratic. Really very hard. Although if you really look, maybe you could find some examples. But yet again the level of corruption depends not on the quality of democracy, but on the public mentality, and their attitude to what is happening around them. And it is anyway pretty difficult to discuss corruption in Arab countries — firstly because the Muslim world remains very closed to us, and secondly because when everything belongs *de facto* to several specific families, and society is ordered on strict class or even caste lines, it is just silly to talk about corruption. There the law dictates that some people have whatever they want, and others have practically nothing, the common people are left with just hand-outs. At first sight it appears that Libya falls out of this list of countries, but I stress that I was speaking only of countries which live according to Sharia law, and the Libyan *Jamahiriya* was never a Sharia state.

Looking at how Russians behave when they are abroad gives us an interesting perspective on our mentality. In fact even the kind of mafia activities which our less upstanding citizens get up to tend to reflect a mentality which is characteristic to Russian statehood. Here we also witness a clan instinct at play, through their efforts to run schemes which allow those on the inside to get away with whatever they want.

I believe our biggest problem is that our laws are no good. If they were better, then the public wouldn't break them so often, and wouldn't moan about them so much. The laws which don't apply to commercial activity are only half the problem. But everything regulating individual relations with the state or with the police is a very real problem. I can't argue with the assertion that one of the biggest issues is that the state has ceased to exist for the benefit of the people. So the phrase which is ascribed to Benito Mussolini — 'everything for our friends, the law for our enemies' — does not really describe Russia. In Russia the law is for no one. In Russia the law as such is more like a stick to beat people with, because the legislative process is entirely incomprehensible, and the way that the law is then applied is selective. In this context, the fact that the court case between Abramovich and Berezovsky is taking place in London, under British law, is a huge slap in the face for Russian jurisprudence. It's just some sort of bad joke. Was it worth spending so many years trying to clean up the legal system if this is what we end up with!

Of course we repeatedly demand that the government behave like the Decembrists, strictly holding them to account for things that we normally forgive ourselves. But it is hard to describe as anything other than a mockery of the law the situation where someone who has taken a bribe of a couple of hundred thousand rubles is detained in a pre-trial detention cell for several months, where he then dies from a heart attack, whereas the former governor of Tula region, who is accused of taking a bribe of several tens of millions of rubles, sits peacefully under house arrest.

We can see these kinds of situations everywhere, because in our country even how the law is applied depends mostly on who you are. It turns out that you can kill a person in a traffic accident if you have relatives in high places. The judges would suddenly notice that you have children, and your sentence would be suspended for 18 years. But if you are doing time for economic crime, and you've got a whole load of small children, and the right to conditional early discharge, then there is certainly no guarantee that you can take advantage of that right, since to the state you are a class enemy.

No surprise that the modern Russian state pursues economic crimes so vigorously, but is so understanding and sympathetic when it comes to crimes against the person. The thing is that for the state crimes against the person are a trifling matter, a minor misdeed, with no direct impact on senior officials, because, thanks to the Federal Protection Service and other special services it is pretty hard to touch them. But an economic crime is an attack on the holiest of holies, on the money belonging to all these officials who are genuinely convinced that everything in the country belongs to them.

CHAPTER 7

Of course the Russian public are tired of putting up with boss's friends. They want to say 'Enough is enough!' every way they can. That is why a number of alternative staff lists appeared to meet the demand for real professionals, from the Presidential Administration to political parties. But when it turned out that the Presidential 100 and the Presidential 1000 looked too much like a life-long reserves bench — because the number of people from this 100 or 1000 who got positions in government was so small — we began to ask whether society's hopes could ever be met.

The call for change has sounded. But what can the system really offer in response? In the Soviet period this demand for change was fed by massive structural work, a whole system of training schools was built under the Party and under the government, including the million-strong Lenin University hated by so many, and the Higher Party School. As well as all these organizations, there was a functioning ideology supporting the training of a new guard. An effective training system was at work which could take a person from a poor family, from a distant village cut off from the whole world, and enable them to rise to the highest levels of government.

Thanks to this 'social elevator' the people who ended up in responsible positions were really ready for it, having climbed all the levels of the administrative and management career ladder, and knowing the work of individual factories, and whole sectors, inside out. It was these people who made up the skeleton of the

Soviet economy: directors of factories, ministers, members of the Central Committee staff. I can't say with certainty that they were all ideologically sound communists, but in terms of the specifics of individual sectors, in particular the military industrial complex, they were experts.

The principle of the rotation of staff existed, which Rashid Gumarovich Nurgaliev suddenly remembered, but which we had otherwise completely forgotten about in contemporary Russia. With all due respect to the former Finance Minister Mr Kudrin, I will note that when someone occupies the same ministerial position for eleven years, like Aleksey Leonidovich (Kudrin) himself, he gets pretty jaded. Rotation of staff is vital, as is the opportunity to work in different regions, so that you get to know our country away from the Moscow-St Petersburg gang, and get a feeling for how much depends on what happens out in the provinces.

To be fair, the government has regularly come to this realization, and tried to freshen things up by introducing a new stream of people. Many of us probably recall those sudden political changes, when half of all the regional governors were swapped all at once, and new people were brought into the government. But these campaigns were sporadic, and emotionally driven, and eventually fizzled out. Yet again many appointments were made not according to professional competence, but based entirely on personal loyalty.

So the idea of a 'big government' announced by President Medvedev generated such a mixed reaction. If at the beginning of discussions there had been some hope that at last expert opinions were going to be heard, many shuddered when someone said at one of the meetings that 'you are all like-minded, and you will form a government which is not just big, but focused on the task.' Because whatever you think of Minister Fursenko — and it is unlikely that there has been a worse Minister of Education in Russia's history — trying to imagine Tina Kandelaki in his place would be enough to drive you crazy. Just like trying to imagine, for example, the talented writer and TV host Sergey Minaev or the wonderful gallery owner Marat Gelman in the place of Minister for Culture Avdeev.

Despite the well-known Russian observation about how it is easy to criticize but harder to propose any action, one must observe that it is not always a good idea for critics to be given the chance to realize their ideas. And the phrase itself, which means in essence, 'if you can't propose anything concrete then don't criticize' is a long way from the truth. In fact when you go to a restaurant and make an order, and you are brought some food which has gone bad or doesn't taste good, you don't actually criticize, you just state the fact that the food is bad. But that certainly doesn't mean that you then have to go to the restaurant kitchen and cook something to eat yourself.

As consumers of government services, we see the results of these services ourselves. And if we say that something is bad it certainly does not mean that everyone who sees it is bad has to drop everything and exclaim that he will come and do it better. This is a really terrifying, dangerous idea. It's quite clear that in no circumstances should we do anything of the sort. What's more, it really is important to be very cautious about new appointments — here I agree with Putin. But — and here I disagree with Putin — not so cautious that we think it is better to work the current officials to the ground, because we don't think they should be replaced in any circumstances. As we know, Putin once answered a question about replacing ministers along the lines that there was no point in replacing them if each time it meant that nothing would happen in that sector for half a year. That is the wrong approach. Or, it's right only if the change means that another outsider comes who begins by changing the whole team. But in reality there should be no upheaval in the ministry, because it shouldn't in any case be a collection of the current minister's friends, but a professionally functioning organization, where there is a clear understanding of who works with whom and on which questions.

But probably the only professionally operating government departments one could name are the Ministry for Foreign Affairs, and the Ministry for Emergency Situations. In those ministries any unprofessional member of staff will immediately be spotted, so the personal loyalty factor is not decisive in gaining promotion until all but the highest positions. But when you see that the appointments in the security ministries, or the main ministries in the social sector are unpredictable even for those of us working inside this country, then you realize that the rule in operation is that you might get promoted, but how far depends first and foremost on who your friends are.

For some reason the government is afraid to death of creating a real professional labor force. In fact, the essence of our approach to fighting corruption can be expressed very simply: 'Beat up your own guys, so that the other guys get scared, don't steal yourself, and don't give bribes to anyone else' — in other words, 'do as I do'. But for all the positive aspects of this approach, it can lead inadvertently to a staffing crisis. It's not enough just to learn to stop stealing. In order for the country to flourish it's also vital to create a functioning system for promoting good staff. This is exactly how the government could show its strength — because a strong government is not afraid of trusting in professionals. But a weak government tries to establish if its officials are loyal to it, sincerely believing that theft isn't a problem if we 'keep it in the family'.

The government begun these tests of class solidarity much earlier than Yeltsin's period of rule. Personal loyalty was important in Soviet times, but class solidarity was even more important. In the early stages the Soviet government understood that it was essential to use the knowledge which professionals could offer, to listen to their opinions, and did not hesitate in inviting both Russian and foreign specialists to come and work, even if they might have had the wrong class background. Typical of this approach was the famous story of how the great German designer Ferdinand Porsche visited the USSR in the beginning of the 1930s and came very close to accepting Stalin's proposal that he head up the whole Soviet car industry. Of course we can't speak in this case of Ferdinand Porsche's personal loyalty to the regime — simply it was clear to the leadership that professionals of that level were needed.

* * *

We speak a lot about professionalism. But where do these professionals come from? It's clear that in any sphere, whether defense, the law, or state administration, people become real professionals only after having gained a certain amount of life experience. But in Russia there are increasingly clans of unprofessional young people in high government positions. And that's without us having experienced anything like the notorious Stalinist purge of the senior officer corps, when young squadron commanders were rapidly promoted to the positions of commander of the air defense armies, which ended up costing lives. We have had no such purges. Just that everywhere 'our guys' are getting ahead. And when they get to positions where they need to take decisions, watched by the people who preceded them who have the professional knowledge, they are possessed by a powerful sense of hatred due to their awareness of their own professional incompetence. Which doesn't result in them trying to learn any more, but the opposite — they try just to survive, driving the professionals out of the system.

But here one should note that, fortunately, this doesn't happen everywhere. There are several vivid positive examples which demonstrate quite convincingly that a strong professional with a lot of experience can not only prove his own professional qualities but bring a huge team of people with him.

One example was the appointment in autumn 2010 of Sergey Semenovich Sobyanin as mayor of Moscow. It should be noted that Sobyanin was in many ways lucky. He was born into a family which understood what it is to work in government service, and has himself travelled a long road — both in his Tyumen region, where he eventually became governor, and during his subsequent work in the State Duma and European parliament, followed by the Presidential Administration and government office. And then Sobyanin came back to work for regional government — this time in Moscow. It should be noted that all these moves from job to job were never accompanied by mass dismissals or large scale purges, nor did Sobyanin bring with him a 'Tyumen team'. As a rule, there were very few people who arrived with Sergey Semenovich in his new positions. If we look at all the appointments which have taken place in Moscow, it is not really possible to accuse the majority of new officials of belonging to a 'Tyumen team' of Sobyanin's. Moreover, effort has clearly been made to treat the city government personnel carefully, no mass purge has taken place of the staff who worked under Luzhkov, no axe is being wielded and no blood is being shed.

Notwithstanding the justified criticism of many Muscovites, it was down to this approach that there was no catastrophic drop in the standards of the city's public service provision during the winter of 2010-2011, which could easily have happened. In any case, the level of dissatisfaction with Sobyanin was significantly lower than with Valentina Ivanovna Matvienko among the citizens of St Petersburg. And this surely can't be put down to a more favorable climate. Rather one should acknowledge Sergey Semenovich's abilities, in taking hold of the rudder at full steam, putting the existing team at ease after the change of mayor, bringing in new people without any conflict or negative impact on work, getting through the difficult Russian winter period without any emergencies, and even trying to relieve the Moscow budget of its awful debt burden. All without any political commotion, without much strong support in the media, all thanks just to hard work.

In this light Sobyanin compares favorably with many other representatives of government, as do Kaluga region governor Anatoly Artamonov, and Deputy Prime Minister and Presidential Representative in the North Caucasus Federal

District Aleksandr Khloponin. These people don't tell the public how they should live and what they should do, instead they show they can listen.

I think that this is one of the main problems with our current government. It doesn't want to listen. It wants only to talk and tell us what to do, which is very dangerous. It means that even when justified criticism is made, and shocking examples of illegal practices are uncovered, there are no changes in personnel. The government acts as if it is scared that if it reacts to public pressure once, it will show it is weak, and will be forced to do so again. In other words what is clearly being demonstrated is an inability to think beyond one's own fears, to answer the simple question: does the signal which is being given indicate a real problem? And if it does, why are the necessary measures not being taken? Otherwise we are not far from an absurd position where it's no longer important whether two times two is four, but who said it — our guy or someone else. But that is an extremely dangerous, destructive way of thinking. The truth should not depend on who says it. It is important to know how to take criticism, even if that criticism is sometimes highly unfavorable.

CHAPTER 8

A career progression structure like the one which existed in the Soviet period, and a genuinely competitive labor force, are essential building blocks in the fight against corruption. But when we consider the various methods which can be used to fight this ill, we can't ignore foreign experience, which can be interesting and instructive.

Having transparent government structures also results in a sharp fall in corruption: when everyone is in full view of everyone else, you won't get away with stealing much. And the media play an important role in shining a light on those who tend to fall into the shadows — not just in the countries which we see as being completely free and democratic, like the United States or Israel, but also in those countries which don't meet all democratic ideals, such as Singapore, where Li Kvan Yu made active use of the press to reveal cases of corruption and other problems. That said, the leader of Singapore fought embezzlement with an iron fist, not just with nice 'civilized' methods.

In America and Israel freedom of the press plays a decisive role in identifying corrupt practices. A large number of big cases are discovered as the result of journalists' efforts, from Watergate to Irangate, or Bill Clinton's problems — and here I'm not talking about his moral failings, but about the corruption schemes which he was responsible for during his time in Arkansas and later as president — following which there was a public call for all possible measures to be taken to prevent such practices being repeated. Barak Obama also has to pay close attention to what the press says. Everyone knows very well that there might be some bias in some publications, and that journalists can sometimes be sacked for their political views, but fortunately there are so many different publications that it is physically impossible to control them all, so there is no way of promoting a single political line.

Mussolini used interesting methods for fighting corruption, which were in many ways close to our approach. So what did the *Duce* do? In the first place, he realized that the country needed money, especially given the social policy which he implemented. So he placed his closest friends in all of the key positions which controlled the distribution of financial resources. But he knew full well that at some point his friends would go bad. So Mussolini set up a secret department of the police which was tasked solely with keeping tracks on his friends, collecting a huge dossier of information on each one of them.

Mussolini realized very well that he needed to create the public image of a leader who was loved by the people. And he succeeded in doing so. It is reckoned that the *Duce* personally provided financial help to two million Italians. Of course, this would have been physically impossible to do on his own — one just needs to work out how much time it would take. So a whole department was involved in this work, reading the letters sent by ordinary Italians and handing out money in Mussolini's name.

Not only did the *Duce* place his people in key positions, but he regularly collected envelopes from them as well. These envelopes took up all the space in the drawers of his desk. And of course from time to time Mussolini's friends thought that the tail had begun to wag the dog, and that he had become dependent on them. But then that special secret police department which I mentioned earlier begun its work. The agents knew everything about Mussolini's friends: who was sleeping with whom, and even exactly when it happened, who was stealing, and exactly how they did it. When their impudence got out of control, there were no loud public court cases. Instead Mussolini would invite his erring ally for a personal chat, unfasten a fat folder and read out several documents from inside it. And after such chats there was not a single case when the friend did not write a polite resignation letter — all of them took exactly this route, disappearing somewhere afterwards. It is interesting to note however that the personal influence of the police chief was very limited. He had great power and influence in his official role, but he also knew very well that he had no chance of arranging a leak of information to the media or of taking a case to court. He had a different job to do.

* * *

Many people think that corruption is a terrible evil and that the absence of corruption therefore means a situation when goodness can shine through. But, as strange as it may seem, one of the least corrupt countries in the world was Libya under the rule of Muammar Ghaddafi. The experience of our fellow Russians who tried to develop the oil fields there showed that the Libyan ministers cared only about the interests of the people.

Ghaddafi was without doubt an international terrorist — we all remember the case of the American passenger aircraft which was blown up in the skies over Scotland. He was of course a tyrant, a despot and a usurper of power, as he tended to be called in civilized countries. Although, to be honest, it is hard to see the activities of these civilized Western countries as wise, or supportive of genuine democracy, when they backed those Islamic fundamentalists and Al Qaida supporters who covered themselves in glory by killing Ghaddafi in captivity and desecrating his corpse, in violation of the Geneva Convention and all ethical norms.

In fact Ghadaffi turned every Libyan citizen into a stakeholder in the oil extraction business, unlike in Russia where after the 1993 Constitution came into force the country's mineral deposits no longer belonged to the people. The Russian people end up with crumbs, in an indirect and opaque form through the government welfare services which are funded by the taxes raised on the oil companies. And what's more, Russians have to pay for these same mineral resources which they don't own when they buy petrol (with taxes added), electricity, and through other outgoings, even if these are allegedly then returned to state sector workers via their salaries.

In Libya the system worked differently. There, just as in the Arab Emirates, and even more directly that in the Emirates, there was a social welfare system. That is why the Libyan *Jamahirija* — a people's republic — was famous for having the highest standard of living in Africa. Genuinely the highest. Young families got government help enabling them to buy a whole house. Ukrainian nurses and Italian professionals were eager to go and work in Libya. And everyone got paid generously. Even the unemployment benefit was several times the average wage in Russia. And there was no corruption. But did this help Ghaddafi hold on to power and, in the end, his life?

It is also common to complain loudly about what terrible things are happening in Italy, and how corrupt that country is. I will remind you, however, that Silvio Berlusconi, who recently departed from office, reached the pinnacle of power on the back of a campaign against corruption. Although he certainly did not lead this campaign himself, he was able to use the media resources which he owned to promote it. This was when the *Mani Pulite* or 'Clean Hands' campaign begun, aimed at fighting the mafia and the corruption which had completely paralyzed Italy. A large number of senators, members of parliament, ministers, and other state officials were squeezed, including Julio Andreotti, who had basically run the country for forty years, during which time he alternated repeatedly between public roles and the shadowy underworld; there were some really major corruption schemes leading right to his door. But Andreotti managed to acquire a status amounting to immunity, and no one would betray him. And in Italy the governments changed so often that there was no sense in trying to remember the names of officials. In the fifty years since the war, the government changed around fifty times — I may be mistaken when it comes to the precise figures, but there were so many reshuffles that it became something of a bad joke.

But despite all of this, who would say that Italy is not a democratic country? Who would say that corruption seriously impeded the development of civil society? Despite the fact that the powerful businesses of the politicians in the South were syphoning off money from the budget to help their regions develop. Yes, Italy was governed for a long time by mafia families, and in some regions they are still in control — the government tries to combat them, often using methods which are far from democratic, threatening family members and confiscating their property on the grounds of suspicion alone, without any investigation or court case. But the whole of progressive humanity remains silent and no one says that democracy is under threat in Italy. Meanwhile the Italians themselves don't think of their country as particularly democratic, and certainly don't believe that there is a low level of corruption there — in fact it is probably even higher than in Russia — and corruption scandals continue to shake the country.

The Italian bureaucracy is in some respects similar to the Russian one. Of course, who you are friends with doesn't play such a major role. Although it is well know that the personal friends of Berlusconi, and before him Andreotti, got to the very top, running the country and taking key decisions, the scale is somewhat different. Berlusconi was in fact a model of incorruptibility compared to Andreotti, even if it would be hard to call him such in any other context. But for some reason we in Russia tend to think of Berlusconi as some sort of black swan, an *enfant terrible* of international politics.

* * *

I reckon it is no mystery why Berlusconi is so popular in Italy. In many senses he mirrors the self-image of the typical Italian — not for those brainy three-percent who get all their news from the internet — but many people were convinced that the prime minister was just like them. They are the people who vote in elections, after all. And which ordinary person would not want to throw cool parties with pretty young ladies when he was already a respectable age. Everyone would, of course! So the Italians would say that he is just like one of them. They also give a thought to God in the morning, to their family during the day, but have nothing against having some fun with a girl in the evening. So what? It's just that he got away with it and others didn't, so they are jealous.

But the main thing, as I have said, is that the Italians don't particularly believe that democratic freedoms are flourishing in their country. They are convinced that the system which exists in Italy is the *'padrone'* system: not exactly the Godfather, more like our merchant class, sort of a father figure and master of the house, who looks after himself, looks after his family, and doesn't forget about the people who are important to him. It was precisely Berlusconi's skill for not forgetting about people that made him very close to the electorate, despite all his faults. That is why the ex-prime minister managed to deftly defuse those bizarre scandals which appeared regularly as if from nowhere. At the end of the day every scandal worked in Berlusconi's favor, because after every one elections had to be held again, and every time the prime minister won once again. So did this mean that Berlusconi understood better than the journalists what the Italian voter wanted?

But did he fight corruption? It's clear that it was pretty hard to tempt Berlusconi with money, since he was anyway so wealthy. This was possibly the main way in which he differed from many of the officials. He was already a more than wealthy person when he came to power. It seems that it is only in Russia that people who are already rich when they come to power still can't resist corruption. Maybe because unlike Berlusconi they mostly earned their money through the businesses of their friends and the friends of friends, rather than by themselves. Berlusconi managed to become very rich regardless of any contacts with friends. As we know, his path to the top was pretty tough — when he started out during his university days he did not shy from earning extra money by working as an entertainer, singing Neapolitan songs on the passenger ferries.

I should stress here that many people in Russia simply do not understand what the politics of foreign countries are like, and in particular how the inhabitants of other countries relate to their rulers — let's take those same Italians and the French for example. It would be pretty hard to name a French president who had not been involved in some sort of sexual scandal. And it's virtually impossible to make the Italian voters indignant about what the international or even the Italian press accuse Berlusconi of. The main thing to stress is that the concept of morality and expectations of politicians differ very strongly between Italy and Russia.

As I have already mentioned, in Russia we tend to demand much more of our politicians and our priests than we demand of ourselves. We want them to be the embodiment of all that is good, everything that we ourselves are not. In many ways we are like those parents who try to realize their failed ambitions through their children. If I did not succeed in becoming a famous footballer, I will take my son and demand that in five years time he is enrolled in the training school of the Moscow Spartak football team, hoping that he will realize my vain sporting dreams. And if I didn't succeed in becoming a great pianist, I will torture my child by dragging him to lessons at the music school every day, and I won't care at all whether he has a gift for music or a cloth ear.

That's exactly how we relate to our politicians. Although we ourselves are, to put it mildly, far from being models of purity and decency, we demand from our politicians qualities that the common man just does not possess. Incidentally, the priest Vsevolod Chaplin proposed a fitting definition of the Russian Orthodox Church, or maybe of religion more generally, during an argument with the journalist Aleksandr Nevsorov, who was hounding him remorselessly, accusing the priesthood of all manner of things, not least because they own all those expensive watches, cars and clothes. Father Chaplin's response was that the Church was a congregation of repentant sinners, who at least recognized their sinfulness. A definition which certainly makes you stop and think.

CHAPTER 9

Is there a single person who doesn't shout about the need for clean elections, or a single member of parliament who doesn't complain about how hard his job is! Is there anyone who doesn't point out how difficult it is to be in politics in Russia, how much work it requires, and how they themselves are honest and clean, it's just that everyone else is evil personified! Our members of parliament know no greater pleasure than rooting out a scoundrel and shouting 'grab him!' And many parties indulge in the entertaining sport of accusing the other parties of being full of scoundrels and thieves.

That term 'party of scoundrels and thieves' became very popular at some point. I will remind you that the first to use it was Vladimir Volfovich Zhirinovsky, and then it was taken up by Aleksey Navalny and made popular amongst those same oligarchs we have discussed. That's pretty funny in itself — even the slogan was stolen! Looks like that's just the country we live in — everyone is on the take.

So Navalny called 'United Russia' the party of scoundrels and thieves. In my view this was highly disingenuous, especially since Navalny was unable to provide any evidence to back these words in a court of law: even Luzhkov himself, for example, has still not been convicted of anything, there is not even a case open on him. I don't intend here to examine the phenomenon of Navalny himself — he doesn't interest me. For me it is no secret, and no surprise, that his popularity has been pumped up using resources which belong to certain specific interests, who are not pro-Putin, but are still oligarchical. If we look realistically at this, then Navalny should have been a bit more precise, and asked whether there is a single party in Russia which is not a party of scoundrels and thieves.

I put this question to the representatives of a wide range of political parties, from pro-Kremlin to opposition, 'name me a single party, which has no scoundrels and thieves amongst its members.' And every time I asked it an awkward silence ensued. Although it really is pretty hard to object to the statement itself. There is no party in Russia which hasn't at some point been caught with its paw in the cookie jar. Moreover, the widespread view that those in power take more bribes often turns out not to be true, and I will explain why. It is true of course that there is nothing sweeter than power. It is also true that every official imagines himself as a little tsar. This bureaucratic phenomenon was described some time ago in the classics of Russian literature, and nothing has changed much since the times of Gogol and Saltykov-Shchedrin.

The latter's Foolsville remains just as it was, only that it has grown to unreal proportions and has long since had a population of over a million. At the same time the fundamental laws of the Russian mentality continue to work just as they always have.

Sure, there are most likely scoundrels and thieves in every party, but no small number of honest and decent people too. And if we look at the statistics, where do we find the most scoundrels and thieves? Are they not in those parties which have to sell their seats to scoundrels and thieves just in order to survive? What kind of honest person would pay from five to seven million dollars to become a State Duma deputy? It's enough to makes you laugh. And if you take a look at any of the parties' list of members, including the opposition ones, then you may get a shock to see the line-up of bizarre characters among their ranks.

* * *

For some reason many people think that the roots of corruption are in the party system, and that if you take one party and purge it, depriving its members of the opportunity of working in government, then goodness and order will reign. This is of course a very naive view, since there has always been theft of public funds in Russia, just that when it was necessary to become member of a party, the officials recast themselves as party members with great ease, acquiring party membership cards with the right names on them, so that they could remain in power and continue with their previous easy business. We call it embezzlement of state funds, they call it, in more affectionate terms, administrative rent. The essence is very simply: if I help you, then of course it is natural to expect something in thanks.

That is why it is very much to the officials' benefit to redirect society's attention away from the system in which virtually every decision depends on the individual preference of a bureaucrat of some grade, towards the members of parliament, exclaiming that they are the spawn of Satan, the embodiment of evil! In any case, many people don't even realize that the laws which are passed in the Duma need the approval of the ministries. Although, on the other hand, this is understandable. Tell me, hand on heart, has any one of you ever tried to read a draft law? Just read it through? And then to understand what it actually says? No surprise that the deputies faces look like they do in the TV broadcasts. I for example like to read books to my children at bed time — it really helps to calm them down. But sometimes I fall asleep after three minutes, and my children start laughing at me, it's all great fun for them. So I know how the Duma deputies must feel — they can't even have a sleep, as they're being filmed. It's pretty tragic. But, joking aside, the Russian parliament, which was anyway pretty toothless, has in recent years been transformed from a machine for stamping laws into something more like an office for handling paperwork. No law will ever see the light of day without the approval of the Russian Government and the Presidential Administration. And the Russian citizens can't comprehend what is going on, and why the necessary legislative changes aren't taking place, after all we are dealing with pretty basic things.

At first glance it might appear that if you are a member of the ruling party, then you have the chance of becoming a state official as well. But you can forget about that! If you look at the officials who become party members, and vice versa, the numbers are pretty small. All the more so if we're talking about high level positions — the only person that comes to mind is Deputy Prime Minister Aleksandr Zhukov, whose personal honesty was never in doubt. The typical official spends his whole career inside the system acquiring the necessary connections, and has no intention whatsoever of giving up the position he has enjoyed for many years, handing over his share of the cake to someone else. He knows very well how the system works, how to make sure that the necessary paperwork is processed quickly, and knows where the tastiest morsels can be nabbed.

That's why I think that Navalny's widely promoted Rospil anti-corruption project is an abomination. It's not enough to scare people and cancel tenders. Sad to say it but no money is recovered like this, the bad guys don't get their just deserves, and the schemes through which the money disappears from the budgets are not discovered. The guilty people are not caught and taken to court, and don't end up in prison where they belong. It all resembles some sort of bureaucratic game of Mahjong — like you're really scared, but it doesn't actually hurt. Someone sets you a puzzle. If you manage to solve it, good, you'll get another harder one. If you don't get caught as you perform the task, you will avoid prison. But even if you are caught, you probably still won't end up in prison, because we're all good guys, and everyone here knows the score. Friends are always nearby so that any dodgy business can be covered up. Although heaven forbid that you get caught during a political campaign — then you will need to take full responsibility, although even then probably only before the media. Everyone will fuss for a bit, they will write all sorts of vile stuff about you, but then some time will pass and you'll see that the problem sorts itself out.

Only in Russia can someone state in full seriousness that the Cherkizov market in Moscow existed completely independently, no one was linked to it in any way, no one had any relationship with it at all, and it was the rector of the Academy for Sports who was solely responsible for the insane volumes of illegal goods being sold. What's the difference if people believed these scandalous public reports or not? It's actually unlikely anyone believed them, after all everyone knows very well that the very same Telman Ismailov probably unloaded suitcases of cash from Cherkizov market on a daily basis, and let's just say that hundreds of thousands of dollars is a conservative estimate for the sums involved. And we can be sure that this money didn't just go to the now former-rector, but to senior Moscow city officials, to the policemen, to the customs service to pay for the hole in the border, and to pay for the protection racket dressed in the uniforms of senior military men. But no one was found responsible. Because everyone was too scared. And before you know it the market was shut, everyone was happy, and the generals and officials all escape prison.

* * *

I have already mentioned the unique court case which was taking place in 2011 in the UK capital, and was still not over as I write. The case is unique because two oligarchs are involved, one of whom who had direct and active involvement in the political life and party building process in Russia. His name is Boris Abramovich Berezovsky, and his role in the formation of the Russian political system should not be underestimated. The other party in the case is Roman Arkadevich Abramovich. He is also a man who is very close to politics, so much so that he was at one time a governor, and even during the court case he was still the speaker of the Chukotka region parliament, although this role never stopped him living in foggy England where he no doubt spent long evenings worrying about the fate of the Chukotka voters.

These two 'respectable' gentlemen decided to tell the whole world about their vile divorce process. And they chose a court in London as their legal battleground, so this is where the realities of Russian political life in the 1990s and early 2000s are being discussed. And the more they talk, the more you get the distinct feeling that all these privatization auctions were so far removed from any concepts of honesty, fairness and the free market, that they were actually one hundred percent crooked — if you believe the representations given in court by Roman Arkadevich Abramovich. The details of the case are both frightening and funny. But the main conclusion which one can make is that corruption is not the right word for what is being discussed. If you believe the evidence given by these men, there is no corruption in Russia at all. Because, as I have already said and will say again, corruption is usually something strange and foreign, whereas in Russia it is the norm of everyday life.

It appears that above a certain level thieving becomes as natural as breathing. And this relaxed breathing, this inability to recognize that one is actually thieving, involves wild sums of money which eventually need to be legalized or at least protected in some way. So it turns out that the most reliable way of protecting and legalizing yourself, if for some reason you can't or don't want to become an official, is to go into politics, notwithstanding the peculiarities of Russian political life and the possible consequences of losing your parliamentary immunity or your status as a member of the Federation Council. All the same, as a Federation Council member with a unique personal background once told me, parliamentary immunity meant only that he had one week's head start so that he could flee the country, if, heaven forbid, he ever had to.

Indeed, if you look at the Duma deputies from all the convocations, all from very different parties, and at the members of the Federation Council, and read up on their backgrounds, then you will realize that for many of them the deputy's pass or the senator's badge is first and foremost a means of making sure that your address remains Okhotny Ryad and not the Matrosskaya Tishina prison. This is why some cases take on such grotesque forms — for example when senator Andrey Vavilov decided that criminal proceedings against him be closed, not because he was innocent, but because the statute of limitations had expired. For Vavilov the status of senator was of course a question of life and death. Much nicer than a spell in a prison cell somewhere.

Duma deputies and Federation Council senators organize investigations into each other's business, just like criminal investigations. Their assistants aren't much different. We have got used to the regular criminal cases dealing with the sale of deputies or senators' seats, but when we you hear about assistants' passes going up for sale you can't help laughing. I've actually always wondered who needs these documents and what privileges they give you. And when you see people who have fought crime all their lives sitting in the same working group as the people who were responsible for that very crime, trying with serious faces to come to an agreement, you can't help being struck by the sad irony of the situation.

* * *

In Russia all the party structures and political life more broadly have arisen out of people's pursuit of personal enrichment. If you think about it, the parties simply don't have the luxury of not selling their seats in one way or another. So if we are going to talk about corrupt scoundrels, we should at least try to understand the thought processes of the party leaders. At some point when you, as leader of a party, begin to think of the costs of the forthcoming election campaign, and you know how much money the state is going to give you towards it, and what your competitors are up to, you realize that in order to make a respectable showing in the elections you have to find a way of getting hold of money. Are you really going to run around collecting party membership fees like during the Soviet times? Two kopecks from the Komsomol members? It might be a sensible idea, but it's never going to happen. Not just never, but no way ever, because there just isn't enough money out there.

Remember the famous joke, when the police investigator asks the rich Russian:

'So you've get eight yachts?' asks the investigator.

'Yes,' comes the answer.

'Six houses?' Yes, again.

'Four townhouses abroad?' Yes.

'And here you've got 104 million in cash?' Yes.

'And is it all yours?' Of course.

'But I've reason to believe that you stole it all from the Russian people!'

'Come off it, how are they going to have that much money?!'

In other words, membership contributions will never be enough to pay for Russia's expensive elections campaigns. Not nearly enough.

That's why the parties are in this situation where they can't publish their papers and can't pay for advertising time, because the official budget allocated to them is too small. What happens next? Well the party leaders sit down at the table and begin to think. Do they need money? Yes they do. But where do they get it from — no idea. Well you could of course take the salaries off all the deputies and use it for the election campaign. But that will still not be enough. If we are talking about the ruling party here, then the situation is much simpler — they have a lot of money. There are always companies or simply private individuals whose sole aim in life is to get closer to power. The party probably has to beg them not to give them more money. But their donors will weep and plead to be allowed to give some more, and most importantly to be remembered for giving it. Because there is nothing sweeter than cuddling up close with the government. You don't want anything in return, you just want to be friends. And that sort of friendship is exactly what leads to the unique make-up of the State Duma and Federation Council.

At one point I was chatting with someone who was not very well know as a Duma deputy, but was otherwise a very flashy young guy, and I asked how he got into the State Duma. He answered honestly that his oil company had helped out the ruling party a few elections ago. And they got six seats for that. They found five people to fill them straight away, and then he decided to go in on the deal.

It's much harder to be member of an opposition party. They know only too well how silly their position is, but they still try to convince themselves that everything is just fine. They still need to try and win the elections and get into the parliament, after all. That's how the party lists end up being populated with major businessmen who have suddenly discovered their communist sympathies, or advocates of the free market who have fallen wildly in love with the ideas of the Liberal Democratic Party, or rich intellectuals who have discovered a yearning for living in a Just Russia. There is some choice to be had, you can pick yourself a party to your taste, and even convince yourself that your views are very close to theirs. So the parties do a bit of trading, not necessarily selling their honor and integrity, but at least a vision of a better life. So when the question of fair elections and getting rid of corruption arises, you need to be clear that change must begin, in the first place, with transparency, and with a realization of the kind of money being channeled into party structures. And then it will become clear why we end up with the kind of Duma deputies which we have.

Trading in votes is certainly not a recently invented form of entertainment. At one point, when the Yabloko party had not managed to get into the Duma on the first round of voting, a sad Grigory Alekseevich Yavlinsky came on to my program and told me that this was the first time that Mr Khodorkovsky had forced him to include a whole group of people in the party list who were ideologically distant from Yabloko — but this was in return for his financing of the party. They were amazing elections, when a manager of Yukos — true a former KGB general as well — suddenly popped up in the Communist party list, and a banker as well. But that is old news now. If you take a look at the latest party membership lists you will find evidence, if not of corruption, then certainly of a marriage of convenience.

Asides from that, a party, even an opposition party, has to find somewhere to sit. If it managed to get into the Duma, then of course it has Duma accommodation. But that's not enough for some. They desperately need to have their own fancy house in town! It's certainly a major, difficult decision to take on accommodation for a long term. And if you work out how much property is owned by which party, across the whole country or just in Moscow, it becomes clear that political parties are actually highly effective business machines. Smaller parties can trade in votes, and do deals, if there is any sense in doing deals with them. Although what sense is there in wasting money on deals with the other parties, when almost everything belongs to just one party? It came as no surprise therefore that after the 2007 elections the main problem which needed to be resolved was the creation a majority ruling coalition in the Duma. Because that would ensure that the money would start pouring in.

Of course you need to contribute a great deal of money or do wonders of party organizational work to end up in one of the top positions in the party lists going into the Duma elections. The days have passed when many respectable people could be spotted in the top ten of the federal party lists despite the fact that their only contribution as candidate was their generous financial support of the party. In the past it was possible to buy seats in the Federation Council for a certain sum of money — which was cleverly called 'regional aid'. Some people found out about the existence of certain regions only once they had taken the decision to represent that region in the elections — before that they could never have dreamed of the existence of these curious places. A couple of short sightseeing trips, using your contacts to meet the local decision makers, and before you know it you're a senator, welcome to the world of politics! These days it's all done in a slightly more sophisticated way. In one of the regions, where a particular party may traditionally be strong, you're given a price in euros for a seat, you're asked to pay half up front, and then a political technologist is brought in, and the campaign is conducted. Sometimes it works, sometimes it doesn't.

* * *

So is this corruption? It's for you to decide. Although ask yourselves what kind of fair elections there can ever be with the current system of party funding? What kind of fair elections can there be if so many candidates are tainted with money from various sources? Right from the beginning they have taken on obligations which are entirely different from those which they officially pledged to their electorate. Some of them will just be happy to squander millions, enjoying the good life, but others know how much money was paid to get their seat, and will begin the painful process of paying it back. And how does a Duma deputy pay this money back? This is where it all starts. Involvement in hostile corporate takeovers, MPs questions — cheap at ten thousand dollars apiece — phone calls to the powers that be. Or you can go and get personally involved, going to obstruct or assist in lawful procedures to seize other people's property. There aren't many people who can resist this kind of pressure. Almost no one. Who wants to get draw in when you're up against a real-life Duma deputy?

We can see with our own eyes that all the deputies have their favorite companies, which they personally look after; parliamentary questions are flying to the Attorney General, or Head of the Investigative Committee, repeatedly from the same senator or deputy, whether male or female. They're showing a real active interest. Making phone calls, attending meetings.

These are all grownups, they all have their system of contacts. No one wants to get into an argument, everyone knows the score. A mutual appreciation society.

Everyone knows the story of how deputy Aleksey Mitrofanov's promised to give the LDPR party two million Euros, and then failed to do so. Such a blatant con made Vladimir Volfovich Zhirinovsky really mad, although, incidentally, he had not bothered to inquire where Mitrofanov had got the money from in the first place. It is well known, after all, that Duma deputies are not allowed to engage in any commercial activities. Which does not prevent them from waging full-scale battles over various pieces of property, as in the case of LDPR deputy Ashot Egiazaryan, who began a fight with another former member of Zhirinovsky's party over that huge piece of real estate, the Hotel Moscow. The affair ended up with Egiazaryan losing his parliamentary immunity and criminal proceedings being started. But the funniest thing was that the fight took place in one and the same party. So what kind of honesty and incorruptibility is possible? And how should we react to the fact that the most 'honest and fair' party in Russia basically has to act as an advertising agent in order to fill its budget, promising all manner of good things with a sly wink, as long as one of the rich kids buys themselves a place in the party list.

One of the most effect methods of fighting this trading in seats, and the subsequent attempts to earn back the costs, as well as the appearance of dubious sponsors within the party lists, is the system of primaries, when one candidate is chosen from the party. The important thing about primaries is that, whether you like it or not, you are forced to explain to the voters who exactly you are, and prove you deserve to get into the party list by fighting for their votes. And not just using money, but the standard methods of politics, by having difficult discussions with the electorate and passing selections processes, because for all the money you might be able to give, it might not help you. Money is all well and good, but what if people simply decide not to vote?

You might come up with the dim idea of buying votes, but it's pretty expensive, all the more so since there are more swindlers out there than decent people, and everyone will try and get in on the game, like the leaders of youth organizations, who will ask for money to deliver voters to you. In short, primaries were created to reduce the number of swindlers and thieves getting into parliament to an absolute minimum. But, as surprising as it may sound, the only party in Russia which conducted primaries was United Russia.

* * *

'There are more things in heaven and earth, Horatio, than are dreamt of in your philosophy.' If Shakespeare had had the chance of spending just a few days in the Russian State Duma, or the Federation Council, he would have had enough material to supply his fans with classics for many generations to come. The complex plots which develop when various groups of deputies join battle to the death can indeed be described as literary classics.

Someone needs to get hold of some piece of business, for example. All that is needed is a planned, coordinated attack. And so the now former-speaker of the Federation Council suddenly announces that the irresponsible owner needs to be deprived of his right of ownership. This revolutionary piece of know-how is supplemented with the details, and it turns out that the problem is not in fact the irresponsible owner at all.

The grounds for the announcement was the explosion in Domodedovo airport. Who was responsible? Terrorists? Come off it. The police or FSB, who failed to prevent the terrorist act from happening? No, can't be as easy as that, although the explosion did take place in the area which the police are responsible for. Let's look deeper, into the root of the matter. Maybe the company behind the airport was responsible for not ensuring security there? Although no one bothered to think how it could have been responsible for security, since it is hard to imagine any commercial organization which would be permitted to conduct the kind of physical searches needed to combat real terrorists. But then how tempting — especially if you take into account that the company was preparing for it' IPO — to declare for all to hear that the irresponsible owner must be seized and punished!

And so deputies questions are sent to the Investigative Committee, and to the prosecutor's office; everyone is making threats and shouting give us the guilty man, punish him, make it hurt as much as possible! And suddenly you see the value of the company fall. And although those particularly enthusiastic deputies don't actually get the full sum of money equal to this fall in value, gratitude is certainly shown.

Actually, the Domodedovo affair had a special one-off price, whereas in simpler cases there is an established rate of payment. It's not unusual for the deputies to have to get by on scraps while they wait for the next big campaign. What rich pickings they had when President Medvedev decided to close down the casinos! As soon as he had signed the orders, people went running to the Duma with trunks full of money. They ran with their eyes popping out to inform the deputies that while the decision to close the casinos was welcome, it wouldn't do to rush it. A bit of prevarication would be well rewarded! So the full might of the executive branch was needed to overcome the sweet smell of money and implement the decision.

Duma deputies are champion writers of all kinds of parliamentary questions. At one point the Head of the Investigative Committee Bastrykin was so fed up with answering all the various missives from the Duma deputies, that he published their questions with their names. True, the outcome wasn't so good. It was clear that this was part of the struggle between the Attorney General and the Investigative Committee, so the blow fell on Duma deputy Aleksandr Khinshtein, famous for his resolute position and active fight against criminals. However, it turned out that Khinshtein was far from the most indignant among the Duma deputies. Lyudmila Borisovna Narusova, famous as a senator amongst other things, stood out thanks to questions which went far beyond what was permitted of members of the Federation Council, and were more than a little strange. In the course of her correspondence with the Investigative Committee, which dragged on several months, Mrs Narusova revealed an amazing depth of knowledge about the details of criminal cases pertaining to certain citizens, and an equally amazing lack of knowledge of the Articles of the Criminal Code and the requirements of the Law on the Status of Federation Council members, which directly forbids senators from getting involved in the 'operative investigations and criminal procedural activities of the organs of criminal inquiry, the activities of the investigators and the activities of the courts.'

I certainly don't want to suggest that what Mrs Narusova got up to was something new. Of course it wasn't, all the Duma deputies fight selflessly for the rights of their electorate, even if the electorate doesn't know anything about it. They help the Russian people. With full dedication to the cause.

* * *

I have never had any interest in looking into the deputies' pockets, it's just that they somehow manage to keep the contents of these pockets permanently on display. They'll tell you, in all sincerity, that they really don't need any official transport, since they have their own which is not too bad. The fleet of cars owned by the deputies makes you feel proud of the achievements of foreign car industries. The thought that being a deputy is not supposed to be some glamorous role, and that they should be a little more modest, never enters their mind.

There aren't that many deputies who are millionaires or billionaires — but they do exist. It's pretty hard to comprehend what they are doing in the Duma. Some of them probably do see the Duma as a helpful stage in their career, or as a way of serving the fatherland, like the deputy Vladimir Gruzdev, who was subsequently appointed as governor of Tula region. Some of them probably just see it as a chance to bide their time in peace and quiet. Some of them may get some sort of buzz out of it. Some of them want to make contacts. Some of them becomes deputies after having worked in commercial organizations, and then before you know it they are trying to secure positions in the ministries, government departments, or parliamentary commissions which have direct influence over the area in which their businesses work.

Here a dilemma arises. On the one hand, it stands to reason that no one better understands the operation of a given branch of industry than those very deputies. On the other hand, knowing the realities of life in Russia, one can be totally sure that if a law on the appropriate level of compulsory life insurance in the transport sector has spent a long time in the Duma without being passed, then this is because a powerful lobby of major businessmen operating in that very sector are trying to do everything possible to protect their businesses from possible losses. It is enough to think of the 'Bulgariya' tragedy, see the payments which were made to the families of the dead, and look at the surnames of the deputies working directly in that sector. And then you see why the law, which Minister Levitin literally begged the Duma to pass, close to banging his fist on the lectern, is taking such a long time to be considered.

After all, in the grand scheme of things corruption is always based on personal interest. And the personal interest of a deputy can always be backed up with the opinion of a larger collective. And everything should turn out fine, after all the deputy is indeed protecting the interests of certain groups. Although at the same time he also does OK out of it, so life can be very, very sweet. Sure, only a very naive deputy can be stupid and crude enough to ask for money, along the lines of 'bring me a suitcase full of cash'. It hasn't been that way for a long time. For ages now it has worked through bank transfers from one unknown offshore account to another, and no one will ever see or suspect anything, so there is no need to put money into a bank deposit box, and no need to humiliate yourself dragging heavy bags full of cash — if, of course, we are not talking about such trifling sums like ten, twenty or even one hundred thousand dollars.

The deputies become heroes in the chronicles of elite society, just the sight of them is enough to bring joy to the owners of expensive Moscow restaurants, and naturally the luxury restaurants in the areas around the Duma and the Federation Council have long since turned into the deputies' eating spots. Each of them has their favorite place, but you still have to understand the psychology of Soviet man — the deputy can't allow himself the luxury of occasionally going to the Duma buffet. That is for his assistants. And the deputy is somehow lonely without the retinue he creates around himself, the higher the deputy's status, the bigger his retinue.

I was always amazed when serious people who already had everything they wanted in life fought like little children upon arriving at the Duma or Federation Council, in order to get a bigger office or windows facing in the right direction. There's something incredibly childish about that kind of behavior-although perhaps it is for the best. At least it is one thing to remind us that they are human.

I have never seen a badly dressed deputy. Or, to be precise, I have seen them dressed with poor taste, but never cheaply. And I'm always so happy for them. Deputies are clearly capable people. Expensive restaurants. Holidays in Courchevel, a parade of fur coats. At one point the head of the Russian state said pretty harshly that ministers shouldn't be seen in Courchevel — it's not right. Russia was going through an economic crisis. But the deputies didn't listen, especially not the senators, in particular the lady senators in St Petersburg who enjoy showing off their fur coats in public. Maybe their sense of hearing wasn't quite as sharp as most people's.

I'm sure that they probably all have their kind sponsors. Many of them have their pet projects which they look after, turning up and getting involved as much as they can. Does this mean that they are dishonest? Of course it doesn't. I'm sure that each of them even has his code of honor. Maybe it's not fully comprehensible to ordinary mortals, but it exists. We all know that when you are close to the people who have influence, it's not hard at all for you to submit the necessary documents. So everything works out just fine! And then the parliamentary term comes to an end, and you have to demonstrate incredible ingenuity, make friends with the party leadership, be seen in all the right places, in order to set yourself up for the next comfortable term. That's probably why it is proving so hard to pass the law on recall of deputies. Because it's just not fair play. You have invested, made a commitment! And suddenly it all gets taken away. It's just not right somehow, not how things should be done.

Sometimes deputies wise up. Sometimes their party is responsible for their enlightenment. Sometimes they get tired of spending money. And they suddenly become amazingly entrepreneurial, before you know it, hop skip and a jump from one party into another. But in this scenario you also need to plan carefully. Otherwise no natural cunning will help you. Take, for example, the well-known political operator, former member of the LDPR party, Aleksey Mitrofanov. A very capable person. But suddenly things started going badly for him financially, and he decided to separate from Zhirinovsky — and judging by the fact that Vladimir Volfovich is still threatening to get him thrown in prison, this wasn't an amicable separation. So he moved across to the Just Russia party, which wasn't very popular at the time. Mitrofanov thought that the LDPR might not get into the Duma at the next elections, because Zhirinovsky had big problems at the time. But a miracle happened! Both Just Russia and Zhirinovsky's party got through. But Mitrofanov himself didn't become a deputy — he didn't get into the new Duma.

* * *

There is not a great deal of public sympathy when it comes to the deputies and their money. On the one hand, everyone wants them to meet the highest standards of probity, and for the money to somehow appear from nowhere. On the other hand, it's not clear what you are supposed to live off when you are in politics. True, the deputies' salaries are not bad, and they get a range of social benefits. Although an income which may look OK from the point of view of an average, or maybe slightly above average Muscovite, is just a joke in comparison with the wealth of many who enter the Duma. Many people say that a State Duma deputy's salary should be lower than it is. But if we pay the deputy a smaller salary, then the only people who will enter the Duma are the rich, for whom the parliamentary salary is anyway meaningless. If at some point the State Duma deputies start to get a decent salary, then it might be possible to attract people who are genuinely talented — if only they could get through somehow. As we have already established, the necessary social institutions, or so-called social elevators, are almost non-existent. One can imagine a situation whereby a young person enters Zhirinovsky's 'Sokol' youth movement, or 'Nashi' or 'The Young Guard', or the Komsomol, and gradually gains experience, doing party work. But then in this case he will have almost no understanding of real life! He will only know about party life.

That is exactly how a whole generation of young people grew up, with entirely different political views, but united by that unique Komsomol glint in their eyes and a passionate desire to run the country. Sooner or later they all begin to talk about how youth politics is vital, about helping the younger party members, and they feel really good about themselves, having already become party functionaries at such a tender age. And they are convinced that the future belongs to them. Their knowledge of real life may be more than limited, but they think that they are already politicians, because they can organize X number of young people, for money or for free, to take part in pre-election events, run around the polling stations, gathering votes. This pseudo political life begins to seem like real politics to them. And so when they at last get into the Duma, amongst the singers, sportsmen, and the oligarchs who have bought themselves seats, they feel pretty confident, but in fact they are just as unprepared for real political life as any other person.

The obvious conclusion is that this system, in which you have to find money any way you can, with no qualms about trading in any resources you may have, pleasing the leader, because that is the only way of getting into the party list during the elections, cultivates in people characteristics which separate our political culture from that of other countries. After all, the attempt to deploy 'Popular Fronts' during the December 2011 elections came from a realization that there is a huge deficit of political ideas, and of new political faces. There are no new ideas, no new people, there is just an awareness of what rich pickings there are inside the system. So that means that when people begin a political career, they already know how the system works, who to be friends with, and how to turn a blind eye to small details. And regardless of the irreconcilable differences between parties, it is clear that deep down they are actually very similar to each other. They all dress so smartly, in such nice suits and shoes, foreign of course. It's almost as if they all get their hair cut at the same place, and they are all so smooth-skinned and alike. And the tragedy of this similarity is that they are happy to slander each other, but are unwilling to answer any questions pertaining to themselves. One result of this is that an awareness of different political platforms does not develop, instead people operate under the principle 'I like it, it's cool' or 'I don't like it, it's not cool'.

As far as fair elections are concerned, I will repeat: first and foremost, free elections start with transparent funding, which makes life much more difficult for thieves and swindlers at all levels of the system. It would also do no harm to change the rules of election campaign funding, by, for example, putting a ban on contributions above a certain level. Neither organizations, nor private individuals should be allowed to pay more than a certain sum — here I'm talking about Russian sponsors, I'm leaving the subject of foreign funding aside. Otherwise there will continue to be gangsters behind the election of mayors and other local positions. If the elections are a success, then they start to carve up who gets what, and they will thieve from public funds with no shame. The suggestion made by many parties that TV airtime and demonstrations should be free of charge has some sense to it. Of course it would make the parties capabilities much more equal. Otherwise financial resources will remain decisive — although without any imagination even financial resources can lead to outcomes which are the opposite of what you want.

The other thing which is essential in order to fix the situation are the primaries which I have already mentioned, under which even the rich candidates can't just bribe everyone left right and center in order to get into the party list. In primaries you really have to work and find out what the main issues are in the region where you are going to campaign, to secure the respect of your electorate.

The third point is of course the principle of rotation. And a clear agreement that no single political force should have a constitutional majority. Maybe legislation should be passed to this end, since only then will the parties begin to subject each other to continuous scrutiny, and there may be some hope of holding them to account.

CHAPTER 10

Corruption is everywhere. There is corruption in the Duma, corruption in the Federation Council, corruption in the courts. Everyone wants more money. Or a favor in return for a favor. Or money and favors. The main thing is that everyone is completely shameless about it. Everyone is on the take, everyone knows how the system works, everyone is trying to redirect flows of money in their favor, and everyone delivers their orders. They all duck and dive to stay in the game. But now we are beginning to fight this. True, it still looks naive, childish even. In other words, we are fighting it, but still not getting too stressed about it.

Recently a close friend of mine phoned me. He said that I would never believe it, but he had just got a consignment that had been through customs, electrical equipment, clean, all above board, officially paid for. Suddenly a bunch of jokers in masks turned up, some sort of customs department investigative department who claimed they had been following the car from the border, that my friend was in receipt of contraband goods, and that they refused to believe the documentation was genuine. So they seize the goods and take them away to their warehouse. My friend asks me for help.

We begin to discuss what happened. Are the documents all there? Yes. All of them? Yes, every one of them. And so what's the problem? The customs service wouldn't believe that the invoice is genuine. But the invoice is present and correct, and comes from a well-known manufacturer. But the customs service still ask us to prove that it is a genuine invoice. So we point to the document — all the bank details, all the necessary information is there. But they still won't believe us. They still had this feeling that something is not right.

So I go to the prosecutor, and complain that my friend is being hassled. The prosecutor writes to the customs service, telling them that the deadline has expired, why can't they return the goods — no criminal offence had been committed. The customs service replies that they have not received all the required documents. They begin to check. The customs service sends the list of documents which they had been given. And indeed, something is missing. So the deadline for the case is extended. Then it is established that in order to extend it, the customs officers simply decided to hide a series of documents which they had confiscated from the company. And they continue their dialogue with the businessman. They are not too rude, but they ask for money. A bit much by today's standards, but they are willing to do a deal. It might be pure nerve on their part, since no crime has been committed, but he can get off the hook for half a million dollars.

But at this point I dig in. I phone my friends, my friends call direct to the head of the whole customs service Andrey Yurevich Belyaninov. He picks up the phone and calls the people who arrested my friend's goods. And on the other end of the line he hears a hysterical voice: they're gangsters, smugglers, murderers, robbers, rapists! In other words the big boss is reporting to his management that my friend is a gangster and robber. To which he is asked if he has lost his mind — these are peaceful law abiding citizens, go and check. So they begin checking again. And someone who is in hearing shot finds out that one of the generals in the security services had decided to do a little business on the side. He just got a taste for it. And what kind of business was this? Nothing major, electrical goods as well. But he didn't want any competitors to get in the way. So, in order to punish the competition he had decided to swipe his goods.

Although not actually take them for himself — that could come back and bite him later — just apply enough pressure so that the competitor didn't get any clever ideas afterwards. Because the goods have already been paid for. So if it was the company's money, then it just meant the loss of capital, if the goods were bought on credit, then the firm has to pay the interest as well. In any case, not too much to be happy about. So the customs officers don't want to give the goods back, again accusing my friend of being a terrible gangsters! A complete joke. We say that we want to have oversight over the ongoing proceedings, and it is granted. And we continue to apply pressure in every way possible in order to establish who has broken the law.

In the end Mr Belyaninov put his foot down, asked his people what on earth they thought they were up to and demanded that they give the goods back immediately. Which was pretty funny for us. But you can't expect people to just work for nothing. They closed the case quickly, and signed the order to give the goods back. Although this was easier said than done. Between the receipt of the first, second and third signatures for the goods to be returned four or five weeks pass. And after the final command to return the goods it suddenly turns out that the warehouse man is ill.

Of course he also has his axe to grind. He apologizes, says he doesn't want to waste our time, but tells us that there is still one small nuance to deal with. We ask in amazement, what nuances there could still be. So he tells us that the warehouse is a private business. He doesn't really care who is right or who is wrong. They have our goods, but want to know who is going to pay for the storage. To which we ask if he has gone completely crazy. He asks us not to get worked up, if we don't want to pay then of course we can take the stuff for free. But it's just that he is ill. And he is on sick leave so he can't come to work. And he is the only warehouse man in the whole world. So he's very sorry, but he may not recover from his illness. Although if we were to accidentally leave a couple of boxes of our wonderful electrical goods behind, then he would be ready to move mountains to get to work, sort out the paperwork and release the goods. But he is not ready to sacrifice his health for nothing.

I'll tell you straight away that I had to force the guy to sacrifice his health, and we didn't leave him anything behind, purely out of principle. But if you think that was the end of it, then you are very wrong. The case was then passed on from office to office, so as to check everything, and then check it again. Because people had been working hard, but hadn't made any money out of it. What a pain. Someone had to get revenge for that.

* * *

Revenge — that is just the right word. It is the way of the modern-day warriors as they fight for their wealth. I can't even say that they are corrupt. It depends on how you define things. Do you know, for example, what a 'good luck letter' is? You will ask what it has got to do with corruption. Nothing at all, in fact. It has to do with good luck. Good luck, for example, is being born a handsome guy in a good family. Particularly good luck is if you, a handsome guy from a good family, end up in the police training school.

Born in a distant mountain village, Gennady Udunyan ends up in Moscow, finishes police training school, and is assigned not to any old place of work, but to the investigative section of the main pre-trial detention center of the Moscow regional Interior Ministry. The young handsome lieutenant goes to work every day, and good fortune awaits him there. He is given the case of the former Moscow district head Yuri Bulanov, whom I talked about at the beginning of this book. No, the case itself is of course not the good fortune I have in mind. He is a former head of district after all, too much attention around him. But it turns out that a whole load of other cases can easily be tied in with the Bulanov case. For example, he was able to open up a new case dealing with the persons unidentified in the original case. There are grounds to suspect that they gave bribes to Bulanov. Or they might have done. Or they might have witnessed other people doing it. So a criminal case dealing with these unidentified persons is needed. And here investigator Udunyan demonstrates amazing powers of deduction — you can see why he became a policemen! He reckons that since his own surname comes from the Caucasus region, that means that if he organizes a raid on a businessman from the Caucasus then of course they will come running to him to do some deal. And so he will play the role of the middleman in a deal which he is in fact making with himself. And for a small amount of money he can hide all the loose ends.

And this is where the 'good luck' letter which I mentioned comes in. It reads something like: 'On the basis of criminal case number XXXX, pertaining to so and so unidentified persons, I require that...' This is then followed by a list of the documents that the unfortunate company must urgently provide. For example, a copy of the documents relating to the company's founding and its regulations; evidence of its registration; evidence of its tax declaration; copies of the balance of accounts; copies of the contracts concluded with other organizations; a registration form for the cash till; the cashier's log; copies of the current account statements; forms showing the cash on account; the turnover balance; personnel lists; labor contracts; copies of mutual credit agreements; a statement from turnover balance; copies of rental and sub-letting agreements....

So the businessman gets this 'good luck letter'. And he begins to count. OK, a kebab seller doesn't have many documents, just three car boot-loads. But if it's a more decentisized business, like a small shopping center, not to speak of the bigger ones, or some sort of factory, then you already need a couple of trucks to transport that mountain of documents. Months are needed to read through them all. In other words the firm's operations come to a standstill for good! But of course senior lieutenant Udunyan isn't responsible for that, it's not his fault, he is just doing his duty. And is happy to stop doing it for a very reasonable sum of money. And since that ethnic group is a tight-knit community, it really wouldn't be expensive. We can come to some understanding. And for those people who don't get it, we can organize for the documents to be seized by force: guys in masks, faces in the mud. And it can all be filmed on a mobile phone and then shown around.

If you take a closer look at his affairs — how lucky it is that his parents are still alive, and that they are wealthy people! It was they, after all, who gave him all those wonderful presents, he didn't buy them himself — the new apartment, the fancy car, itself a clear give away because it isn't Russian-made and no way could a police lieutenant normally afford it, not even a senior one. Of course we all agree that it is just good luck. Complete luck. But a great number of people had to get involved, some of them very senior, just to get the lieutenant dismissed — and he got away without any more serious consequences.

Dozens of businessmen suffered at his hands. Some of them just paid up in order not to get trapped, knowing how things work in Russia. Some of them tried to put up a fight, but that just made things worse. A large scale operation had to be conducted in order to clean out this filth. And at the systemic level, the magic formula 'pertaining to unidentified persons' means that anyone in uniform can kill your business forever just by seizing the documents. And you just have to put up with it. How wonderfully it all works for them! Just open an investigation into Evroset telephone company. Before you know it, their share value falls, you arrest some of their people, and the owner realizes that it's time to sell. Who cares that the case then collapses in court, the people turn out to be innocent, and the state has to pay them compensation? It's the state that pays, not the policemen who sit in their stations.

* * *

In recent years I have pretty much become an historian of the battles around Domodedovo airport. It's really interesting, because it seems like almost everyone has tried to take control of

Domodedovo at some point. I'll say a bit more about the famous case investigating the 'failure to meet the required standards of transport security'. The suspicion has already fallen from the main actors, and the case itself has been transferred from the main Investigative Department of the Russian Federation to the district level, where Major of Justice Knyazev is now dealing with it. I want to talk about him separately, because Major Knyazev is a complete genius, having devised a completely new method for winning cases in the arbitrage courts. I really think he deserves a medal for it.

And so, on the evening of 1 December 2011 they turn up at Domodedovo again to conduct searches. The Investigative Committee pretended that it was still looking into the transport security case after the January terrorist attack. But I had the feeling it was holding something back.

I managed to get sight of an internal document — the court order authorizing the search at Domodedovo. And I was stunned by what I read. Judge for yourselves, the first sentence read as follows: 'On 24 January 2011 Evloev blew himself up in the airport building. Thirty seven people were killed.'

And the second sentence — just follow the logic: 'Therefore it was requested that it be established in the course of investigations whether Domodedovo's appeal to the arbitrage court with an action against Vnukovo airport relating to fuel supply (for X million rubles) was legal.'

I'm quoting from the text of the document here. Major of Justice Knyazev's signature is at the bottom, and it is he who came personally to the airport with the warrant that night. You will recall that the famous Sherlock Holmes in Conan Doyle's books used cocaine, or was it morphine, but basically he was a bit of a drug addict? Judging by this document, the Investigative Committee agents really give Sherlock Holmes a run for his money. Not in their powers of deduction, unfortunately, but then who needs deduction when you've got your seniors' orders. But what is really interesting is what kinds of mind-expanding substances they must be using. The cynicism knows no bounds. What Major Knyazev wrote basically translates as the following: 'Evloev killed thirty seven people and by doing so handed the Investigative Committee the excuse to meddle in all aspects of the airport's operation, which is exactly what the Investigative Committee now has the pleasure of doing.' It's only a step away from Major Knyazev writing his next search warrant to read: 'Thank you, Evloev, for making this possible.'

I see the situation as follows. The criminal investigation began ten months before that warrant was issued. Very little time at all was needed to deal with the questions relating to transport security. It was quickly established that the transport security requirements were not based in law, and so the case began to fall apart. They then began to look for the airport shareholders, using search warrants. They found some shareholders, but not others, and so decided that since the court case was anyway under way, why not use the opportunity to resolve a few other issues.

So they dug a bit deeper into the Domodedovo case. And it turned out that there was an ongoing arbitrage case between Domodedovo and Vnukovo involving a sum of one billion rubles. You would have thought that if an arbitrage case was under way you would leave the court to deal with it. All the more so since Vnukovo's interests were being represented by the respected law firm Musin and Partners. Valery Abramovich Musin, in case anyone doesn't know, is a Fellow of the Academy of Sciences and a former teacher of the current Russian president from Leningrad University. He is also a member of the Board of Directors of Gazprom, and a member of the Higher Qualifying Collegium, in other words he is involved in the appointment of the arbitrage court judges. Surely his firm could handle a trifling arbitrage case? But I'll let you into a little secret. A legal firm is all very well — but not if your opponent has some serious documents he can deploy.

All of a sudden, one week before the sitting of the arbitrage court, the Investigative Committee asks the question out of the blue: was Domodedovo's arbitrage action against Vnukovo legal? And they turn up with a search warrant at Domodedovo, to seize all the documents relating to that arbitrage case, and the computers into the bargain. How do you like the sound of that? A police raid. Someone appears in court — that's the clean part of the work. Someone else guts the safes of documents at night — that's the dirty part. Kind of front office and back office functions both at work. And in whose interests? Well, that's the most interesting bit! Where did the investigators go with their arrest warrant? You will never guess — to the solicitors firm which was handling the airport's business.

It may not be immediately apparent, but Major Knyazev actually managed to carry out a constitutional coup. The law says that the search of a solicitor's office can take place only with the sanction of a court, no other way. That's a sacred principle. So Major Knyazev arrives in the middle of the night, without a court decision, and informs the solicitors that they will do the search right away, and go to the court later. Although it's not too surprising, since it's a kangaroo court anyway.

Proper lawyers may not believe that this actually happened. But I have at my disposal copies of Major Knyazev's warrant to search the solicitors' office. I reckon that the management of the Investigative Committee need to organize a campaign to tackle ignorance among their staff. And, incidentally, company raiders should take note. Major Knyazev of the Investigative Committee invented a very effective means of winning in the arbitrage court — all you need to do is turn up at the solicitor's office of one of the parties, seize all their documents and computers and seal up their office. I wonder if the Major also thought up some ways of perfecting his scheme, to somehow get the solicitors themselves out of the picture as well? But in any case, without their documents and computers the poor guys couldn't do much anyway.

And so there was this refueling company at Vnukovo airport. It had debts to its creditors amounting to 128 million. The court decision came into force. And that refueling company just evaporated into thin air. The same people are sitting in the same place, with the same kerosene, but now under a different company's sign. To put it simply, they were dumped by Vnukovo's creditors. But for some reason the Investigative Committee is not going there to search anyone.

So that's how talented people operate. But after that how can we speak of an impartial court and investigative service? And what on earth is going on anyway?

As a follow-up, here is another story — a sad one. Under Russian law, aerodromes belong to the state, and that includes Domodedovo. The airport and other services can belong to private operators, but the most important stuff, the runways and the special equipment are federal property. In Domodedovo there is a state enterprise which is called 'Domodedovo Airport Administration', and the federal property is on their balance sheet. Until Spring 2011 the director of the company was Leonid Semenovich Sergeev, a legendary man, a real professional, decorated by the state for his services to the transport industry. He belongs to that generation of men which is now disappearing into history. Sergeev came to work at Domodedovo in 1966, as it was being built, and in 1991 he became the boss. All together he had worked at the airport for 45 years, he had witnessed the birth of Domodedovo, its rise, its collapse in the 1990s and its rebirth under the new team. At the end of the 1990s Leonid Semenovich had the guts to come out in support of bringing a private investor to the airport, and he implemented that plan. At that time he was all but accused of treason. We all know what the outcome was.

Following a terrorist attack in January 2011, the Investigative Committee initiates criminal proceedings against the airport. In February the Attorney General's office joins in with the latest inspection, and in March of the same year Leonid Semenovich dies. He was seventy three years old.

Here the Investigative Committee in the person of the very same Major Knyazev turns up, with a document stating the following: 'According to information at the disposal of the Investigative Committee, the Director of the Federal State Unitary Enterprise 'Domodedovo Airport Administration' Sergeev has died. It is therefore necessary to organize a series of search operations and establish the full details of Sergeev's close relatives, and the real estate, property and vehicles owned by Sergeev and his close relatives over the last thirty years.'

Major Knyazev is completely inscrutable. I again recall Sherlock Holmes and his fondness for both the violin and morphine. What he plans to look for — investigator Knyazev, not Sherlock Holmes — has no legal significance. No one, including Knyazev himself, could explain what he is going to do with that information. Any of the solicitors, whom Knyazev is so fond of searching in the middle of the night without court sanction, could tell you that the relatives and their property really have nothing to do with it. It's clear that the Major was given a task just like in the fairy story: 'Go over there, not sure where, bring that thing, not sure what.' They sent him to Domodedovo, but didn't explain what he was supposed to look for. And so he tries to perform his duty in so far as he is able, and with him 15 guys all looking identical, from the Investigative Committee. And the police officers too. And all that at tax payers' expense, naturally.

* * *

Can everything I have described above be called corruption? Decide for yourselves. But how many respectable law enforcement officers do you know who manage to live off their salaries? At this point you normally hear that fairy story about how once upon a time in far off parts, there lived a fabled hero who didn't take bribes. I won't argue that this never happens. But the public can't be conned that easily, we have all heard too many stories about how respectable representatives of respectable professions turn crooked. When the generals of the Investigative Committee issue threatening ultimatums from one businessman to another, and get involved in the flotation of private companies, and the proud public prosecutors sing songs from the criminal underground in unison at their birthday parties, fully paid for by the quiet and modest businessman working in the gambling sector — that is all our reality. If anyone thinks that the Moscow region casino business is unique — don't kid yourselves. It's clear that in every region the guys working in the state security apparatus have different areas of business which they specialize in, but wherever they are, they don't do badly out of it.

But then they're all grown-up people. How can they live any other way? It's impossible of course. They need to feed their families. And to make sure that you don't fall victim yourself, you need to be friends with your neighbors. And to make it easier for the neighbors to coordinate their activities, the strongest one takes on the role of godfather. A gangster in uniform. And you definitely need to be on good terms with him.

I spoke with Aleksandr Gennadevich Khloponin, while he was head of the North Caucasus Federal District. He told me that if all the law enforcement officials behaved decently, then there would be no problems at all. But instead, wherever you look there are lads from Chechnya with official ID, who don't know how to behave themselves. If the police from Stavropol, Krasnodar and the other regions were not afraid of tackling all the criminal offences, regardless of rank and ID, then everyone would be as good as gold. But the problem is that everyone is too afraid to do anything.

To get public office you need to pay, and pay well. I once got a call live on air from someone who described how a policeman paid to get his commission renewed, and how much he paid, and I realized that when these people get into the law enforcement agencies, their first task is to try to win respect. It's business, nothing personal. The guys need to learn how to get by in that environment. And quickly. You really believe that you're doing nothing wrong. It's just the country we live in! Just look at how the neighbors are living. That police general, for example, has got an Olympic-size swimming pool, and a huge castle. But he's a general! Why should it make people indignant? If he were just a lieutenant, you could say that he'd been greedy. But a real life general! Is he supposed to live in a hovel or something?

Of course the state could easily tackle these problems. But then what would happen next? Is someone going to work for the salary which law enforcement officials get? What quality of person would we get? Let's say we gave them a massive pay rise. We would probably get better quality people. But some time will pass, and then the key question would be whether this means that the law begins to work without a hitch? I doubt it. We don't respect the law in this country, and we have a complex relationship with corruption. Of course all those corrupt people are scoundrels, scum, pigs. But we are just as able to do engage in corrupt dealings if we need to. How else is it possible to work in this country? Let's say you really need some document. Are you going to go and wait in a queue for hours? Is your time really worth nothing at all? There's your answer.

Corruption is a way of life for us. It is what makes us who we are. Manifestations of corruption can be found everywhere. And we don't find all of them annoying. Only where someone is taking more than they are entitled to. But we're understanding towards all the other cases.

That is why Zhirinovsky's idea about legalizing bribes and forcing people to pay tax on them was pretty popular with the public. But if we leave aside the intended shock value, the introduction of payments for the speedy completion of documents or sale of nice number plates in the State Automobile Inspectorate would allow us to tackle the low-level corruption, but it will not solve the fundamental problem. The problem is, I repeat, that society does not see corruption as a terrible evil. It is a problem which bothers everyone a bit, but it remains pretty intangible. In other words, we deplore corruption but we perceive it to be happening somewhere else, with other people.

And when we use the term corruption we don't mean whether someone got their money honestly or dishonestly, just that they are getting indecently rich.

* * *

Probably one of the fundamental principles of the Russian people is a dislike of people who get too big for their boots. We just can't stand it. So when we see someone like this, we are just waiting for them to fall. Just so that we can then say look, I told you so! Corruption means that we see too many people like this. I don't think that the most corrupt person in the country — although it's not clear who he is — is hated as much as Abramovich. The main thing is that he has got money, and you haven't. That is what people probably can't forgive. What's more, in Russia there is traditionally a strong feeling that it is impossible to earn money — there is even a saying: 'You will never earn from honest labor.' So all you can do is steal. But what is amazing is that as soon as someone starts trying to fight corruption it turns out that this itself is also a form of corruption. Every time that someone declares that they are clean, the public takes one look and tells them they must have gone crazy, there's no chance.

So the corruption of the police, the Duma deputies, the senators is first and foremost linked to a mental, or moral corrosion, to an entirely wrong approach to life. In a situation where your ascent of the career ladder depends not on your professional qualities, but rather on your friends and family, you have no real motivation to serve the people. After all the reason why the notorious Denis Evsyukov rose up the ranks was certainly not that he was a good policeman. He just came from the right family. No surprise that Moscow police chief Vladimir Pronin lost his job after Evsukov shot those unarmed citizens. The thing is that even when he was reporting about the situation to the President of the Russian Federation, the Supreme Commander In Chief of the armed forces, Pronin said with complete sincerity that 'on the whole Evsyukov was a first rate policeman, but he had a mental breakdown.' The consequences of Major Evsyukov's breakdown was the shooting of those innocent people. In fact, even his dismissal worked in Moscow's former police chief's favor: he was appointed vice president of the State Corporation 'Olimpstroi' and as far as I know this sorted out his financial affairs in a flash.

CHAPTER 11

I recently spoke in front of an audience of readers at the biggest Moscow book shop. As is often the case, the conversation turned to television. A sturdy looking old man told me that there is one subject which would give me really high ratings. When I inquire what that might be his reply is, believe it or not, gardeners. My skepticism prompted me to ask what the deal was with gardeners. His reply was that he had met the head of the Moscow region police, who had told him that there are millions of rubles at stake in gardening.

It sometimes seems to me that all these stories about corruption are beginning to resemble the legends of the South American Indians from the Amazon river basin. One time a very intelligent person came on to my program, who had spent his whole life researching lost and forgotten tribes, who speak very rare languages. And what he said was very interesting. Turns out that this one tribe has the word 'Jew' in their language. During the Spanish conquest, the most frightening thing which the Christian priests could mention in their conversations with the Indians was Jews. The thing was that the Spanish had tried to convert these wild tribes to Christianity, and had told them the gospel in their own words. An image of a mysterious, wild and frightening foe, who in fact no one had seen, was formed in the local consciousness, and the word Jew came to be used to describe anything that was really bad.

So sometimes it seems to me that the word corruption is used to describe all sorts of different things Russia, even if we don't really know what we are talking about. Corruption can be anything which damages the system, from dumb embezzlement of public funds and theft, to the use of public office for personal gain. Stagnation, the absence of political competition, the extreme shortage of professionals — we treat all these things as different aspects of corruption. It's not that the word corruption sounds as scary to us as the word 'Jew' does to the Amazonian tribes. But we have got used to describing anything negative as corruption. Anything we are not happy with. So there are bad, corrupt people all around us.

* * *

It's probably that this is just the kind of people we Russians are. We have always lived in the name of some kind of ideal. So if in the 1990s the main idea could be summed up with the slogan 'Do whatever you can to get rich!' and success came to be measured in purely material terms, could we really demand of people that they did not take advantage of the opportunities for getting rich? After all, as the ongoing legal process between Abramovich and Berezovsky shows, you don't need to be clever or talented in order to become impossibly rich, you just need to know how to use your connections. That's corruption for you! Turns out that you can grab a huge oil company for a fraction of its true price, in complete contempt of the law. You can then turn legal. You can dump your closest friends and teachers. You can become a regional governor, or whoever you want, without a higher education, if you want to. Money decides everything. No one asks whether this is honest or dishonest, these categories just don't exist in Russia! No one says: 'look, what an honest man.' Instead they say: 'what a pleasant looking man, he looks like he has done well for himself.' But no one feels comfortable asking questions. Because in response you get the hissing rebuke: 'Get off my case, you're just jealous, everyone lives like this!'

The citizens of the Soviet Union knew that anyone could be arrested and stitched up at any moment for anti-Soviet activities, but these days it's possible to arrest anyone you want and find them guilty of breaking some law or another. Either someone gave someone a lift in his car and didn't pay tax on the money he earned, or someone nicked a part from the factory and sold it on the sly, or they decided to take a little something home with them. I'm not even going to mention the intelligentsia — university teachers for example. One favor there, another favor here. If you think about it, how is a teacher going to feel if their official salary is so small that any postgrad student, especially if they are paying fees, is better off. Here we see class hatred getting out of control. So often the bribes which the teachers take are intended not just to give them the minimum income required for a decent standard of living, but as a form both of self-humiliation, and of humiliation of the student, showing him that despite all his money he is still basically an animal who is not capable otherwise of passing the subject. If you are so rich, then you can pay for the reports and exam results!

This leads to real corruption in our higher education establishments, and the real reason for this corruption, I repeat, is not so much material as moral. And it is surely going to have a negative impact on our country's future. Yesterday's students, with the diplomas they have paid for, enter real life as uneducated, unprofessional people — although they do understand that the money they or their families paid is some sort of investment which they have to earn back. That's what they have been taught! A purely commercial approach. And what does this mean if you are a dentist or surgeon? You might make your money back, but you have no medical abilities! All you have demonstrated is that you were capably of buying your diploma.

The situation on the roads in Russia gives us a vivid example of the true nature of corruption. Due to corruption, road building costs absurd sums of money, shamefully little of it is done, and corners are always cut. Then people with their driving licenses obtained with bribes drive on these roads, without being properly taught how to drive, so the result is that every year we lose 30,000 people in traffic accidents — the population of an average Russian town — and there is no end in sight. This is without doubt another impact of corruption.

And what about our health care system? If you have no money, it is basically impossible to get treated. Even if you have the right to a state-provided operation, then, firstly you will have paid a price for it, and spent plenty of time and effort getting it as well, and secondly, the nurse looking after you after the operation won't give a damn if you are paying or non-paying, she needs money to live as well. Try and get your elderly relative into a decent hospital without paying for it! It's been this way for some time now — however famous you might be, any dealings with our medical system are much easier if you have a wad of money in your left hand, and a drawn sword in the other. And just try turning up without one of the two — no one is even going to talk to you. Should we call this corruption? We sure should.

But you could take a different view of the situation. Maybe all of this is not in fact corruption, but just a new type of state. And a new form of public consciousness. That is why we can't tackle it, because things are actually much worse than we thought. Normally, corruption is something alien, foreign to the system. But maybe for us in Russia corruption is not the cancer, but the actual cells of the body themselves. Maybe we have become completely transformed, and there is nothing to worry about. Maybe from now on we should just see corruption as a way of life — something we need to keep in trim like a fast-growing head of hair, cutting only the hairs which stick out most obtrusively.

* * *

After all, it's not possible to transform the country overnight. And anyway, several generations are basically already lost. Moral standards differ so strongly between different parts of society, but also within the individual strata. Our ability to orientate between concepts of 'good' and 'bad' has disappeared completely. Even amongst the predator class amusing things have started to happen, when certain characters lose touch with reality and betray their own kind, biting the hand that feeds them and getting carried away by liberal delusions. Mr Prokhorov is one of the most amusing recent examples of this in the political sphere.

The case of Mikhail Prokhorov is a serious subject which in many ways links in with the theme of corruption, because it reflects the public mentality in today's Russia. The project itself seemed to have been conceived by clever people, who understood that a party on the economic right was needed in the country. Great efforts were made to identify and put forward people who could represent this position. Ministers and members of the Presidential Administration were put forward as candidates, but it became clear that you can't just pull the wool over clever peoples' eyes, if they know the rules of the battles going on behind the scenes. Anyway, is it as easy as that to take on the leadership of a political party? I think not. It also means losing the ear of the president or prime minister. And as soon as that happens the fate of angels befalls you: as we know, angels have high rank, but their strength depends completely on their proximity to the throne. The more light is shone on them, the stronger they become. The same with officials — it's not important what your position is, what is important is how many minutes you have the bosses ear each day. But if you lose this access you are never going to meet just by chance, so your influence falls hugely.

And then they decided to bring in Mikhail Prokhorov — he seemed at first glance to be a clever, decent kind of guy. He should have been easy to control, ready to reach a deal, and with his height he could be seen from a long way off as well. And he seemed unlikely to show any initiative himself, asides from in his endless quest for having a good time. But then problems started happening. Having become the hero of the story, Prokhorov began to believe that he was not just working to orders, but had a free hand, even if this was never part of the original deal. In Russia, once they get some position and are given their orders people tend to get carried away, and believe that they are free to decide what to do from then on. All the more so if they are paying. Prokhorov thought that since he was financing the party and it was his face on the posters, then he could hire his own political advisors, and do whatever he wanted. He thought he had the right to bit of freedom of maneuver! But he completely forgot that in Russia the position speaks louder than the money.

As far as money is concerned, I heard the following story, no doubt made up. In a far away kingdom, a man got on the wrong side of his boss, who was dearly loved by all. And this man behaved badly. Really badly. Eventually he ended up in court. So he sends a courier to the judge with a suitcase full of money and the message 'you know what to do'. The judge takes the suitcase and promises that whatever the evidence, with this kind of money victory is certain. But in the morning the middle-man gets a call asking him to come back to the judge. When he arrives, the trembling judge gives back the suitcase and offers to give him another one as long as the courier forgets that he ever came to see him.

The moral of the story: not everything is decided by money in Russia. Sometimes a phone call is even more important.

You can have any amount of financial resources at your disposal, but there is one important difference between the hot line to the Kremlin and the *Vertu* mobile phone. Your *Vertu* may be made from pure gold, covered in shiny diamonds, you may need to keep it in the safe of a Swiss bank, guarded by soldiers with machine guns. But when you get the call, it turns out that what is important is not the make of phone in your hand, but what number is calling. And the man who doesn't give a damn how many carrots your gold is or how many zeroes are on your bank balance will tell you in a quiet voice to come round and see him. And you will come running to his office in the Kremlin, tail between your legs and your diamonds well hidden. And there it turns out that even if you thought you were two meters five centimeters tall, your height is now only one meter twenty centimeters. Just try and say otherwise, or misbehave in any way. Suddenly you will find yourself shrinking. You get smaller and smaller, and you longer have your own party, you are just a nobody. Maybe somewhere out there you were a really big guy, but not here...

The well-known Jewish joke from the Brezhnev era comes to mind. At one point Leonid Ilich decided to get himself a suit made. He chose a three meter piece of material, but the Kremlin tailor tells him that it is not enough, he clearly needs more. And then he goes on a trip to Odessa and visits the local tailor's shop, telling them that he's got three meters of material, can they make a suit? The tailor readily agrees, just that there is rather a lot of material, so he will make a suit, some Easter trousers, a waistcoat, and there will even be enough left over to make a little cap. Brezhnev points out that in Moscow he had been told that it wouldn't be enough material. To which the tailor replies that Brezhnev might be a big man there in Moscow, but that here in Odessa he shouldn't get any ideas.

So the situation repeats itself. You might be big and scary in the world of business, but here...here the mice will devour your party, and all your sloganeering and attempts at wheeler dealing are worth nothing. Here you'll be asked in a surprised tone who it was that you said you did a deal with. In the same way that parents would ask their five-year-old child, who has just swapped a bicycle for some pebbles: 'What? What did agree with that little boy? What promise? Let's go and see his parents!'

So it turns out that your words are worth nothing, and all the deals you have done are worthless too, and the only person you're scaring is you yourself, and the more you frown the more it looks like you want to fart. At first you might arouse pity, but after that no one really cares. For one reason: if you want to become an opposition politician, then go and be one! But if you first come and kiss the hand of the Kremlin, your height will be no greater than the distance from the floor to the finger bearing the ring, which is not very far. So don't show off, just do as you are ordered. Or otherwise don't go to the Kremlin, don't meet with them, don't bow to them, don't profess eternal love — instead build your own political career. But you wanted to beat everyone else! You wanted to buy your way up. You wanted to do a deal. This is all another manifestation of corruption. But suddenly it turns out that it doesn't work.

...When this book was already nearly finished, some sensational news appeared in the media: Prokhorov had just put forward his candidacy in the presidential elections. I have to say that there is one aspect of this man which I find fascinating: I have no idea what he is thinking. I mean that his thoughts are a complete mystery to me. Especially if you take into account that before putting his name forward he praised Putin and said that there was now no alternative to him. After all, on 9 December you could hear on the news: 'The ex-leader of Right Cause has announced that there is now no alternative to Vladimir Putin as candidate for the Russian presidency.' In his blog in *LiveJournal,* the businessman wrote: 'Like it or not, Putin is currently the only person who knows how to run this ineffective state machine.' And literally moments later, on 12 December, we learn that having stared into the mirror for three days, he had found an alternative to Putin — it's him!

People are asking now if Prokhorov is going to merge forces, as his party did. No, it looks like he is going to do things differently this time. I'd like to know if he is going to have the same crack team of political advisors. Don't imagine that I'm against all this, I'm in favor, let everyone who wants to put forward their candidacy for president. I'm just interested in whether he can collect enough signatures to take part without using administrative resources, or to put it more simply, without ordering the workers at his factory to vote for him? Or is this just the latest Kremlin wheeze, and in a few months time

Prokhorov will sob that nasty Surkov didn't let him take part in the presidential elections? I'm also interested in how he is going to organize his campaign this time. Because Prokhorov has one giant minus against him: the elections take place during the skiing season, and Mikhail was always honest about not wanting to change his lifestyle for anything. So I'd like to see how he plans to take part in the debate. But, as they say, we will have to wait and see.

* * *

The tragedy of all corrupt people is that their wellbeing and their greatness depend entirely on the positions which they occupy. And occupying these positions depends on their ability to deliver on a number of deals, which might all be very different in nature. They might be financial deals — paying a certain amount of money roughly every month. They might be personal deals. Any kind of deal. But these deals will always be there, and you are always obliged to deliver on them. You always remain part of the system, and part of society. A corrupt person can never exist alone, after all. So when those brave people who are fighting corruption single out just a single person it's not just funny. It's hilarious. It means that in recent times all the corruption cases have arisen deep public antipathy. The Russian people are clever, you can't con us that easily. Clever, because in the depths of our hearts we know that we are all just the same. If you put any of us in the same situation, we will start thieving as well! At first in moderation, with a conscience. But then — as much as we can get away with!

CHAPTER 12

Before the recent elections a great number of politicians spoke on the theme of corruption. Almost all of their campaign speeches referred to plans to tackle corruption, described corruption as a terrible evil, declared that corruption must be eradicated, and so on. But for some reason it was hard to believe them. For example Sergey Mikhailovich Mironov said that we need a government of professionals in order to prevent corruption. So I asked him to name his candidates for the government. And he answered that Elena Drapeko would be Minister for Culture, and that someone from the paratroop forces would be Minister for Defense. So everything was immediately clear. Esteemed Mrs Drapeko is a member of the same party as Mironov, who himself once served in the paratroop forces. But is that really enough of a basis, using the criteria of personal acquaintance and previous experience, on which to choose a professional for the role? One could argue that this approach in itself creates the preconditions for corruption.

After all, corruption is not only about stealing state funds. Corruption lies in the fundamental message which is sent when the law applies differently to different people. As soon as the law starts to be different for different people, the ground is clear for all manner of evil doing. And I mean evil, because there is no other way of describing it. When two people commit one and the same crime, of the same degree of seriousness, and one person is sent to prison, and the other is patted on the head and appointed to a new job, then everyone will draw the obvious conclusions and will remember that this was allowed to happen. But if this was allowed, then we have to understand exactly why.

There is clearly truth in the ancient Eastern saying that a country lives happily when its wise men set a good example. Otherwise, you can repeat the word 'halva' as many times as you want, but you still won't get a sweet taste in your mouth. If I can see that the events going on around me resemble more and more the Gianni Rodari fairy story 'Jasmine in the country of liars', then I will have no faith in the law. And what right do you have to try to make me ashamed that I don't live according to the law, if you yourself do not do so? You might threaten me, and tell me that I will feel the full wrath of the working people. But then you and your relatives got away with it!

This concept of the law being the same for everyone is entirely new for Russia. Of course, over the last decades everyone has been busy declaring that there is one law and that everyone is equal before it. But in reality this equality never existed in Russia. That is why corruption is an inseparable part of our national character. It can manifest itself in a number of different ways: either in the form of embezzlement of state funds, or in a strong desire to help our nearest and dearest — but in essence these are all caused by the absence of equality before the law. After all, we did not even have the concept of citizen for a long time. We had a class system, headed by the nobility. And this system in itself implied inequality.

There is a well-known historical anecdote about how the Prussian King Frederich decided to demolish a water mill belonging to a peasant. 'No, your highness,' the peasant objected, 'you can't destroy my mill. In Prussia we have judges as well. See you in court!' And the king was forced to back down.

Could such a story have happened in Russia? No chance. In Russia everything basically belonged to the Emperor, and everything was decided by the nobility. We have always depended on the good favor of the nobility. But you have to choose between relying on the kindness of the nobility or the fairness of the court. You can't have it both ways. You either have the will of the Emperor, or the letter of the law. We have had a saying about the law since time immemorial in Russia: the law is like a pole dragged by horses — wherever they turn, that's where it goes. Not because we had a negative attitude towards the law. It's just that right from the beginning we didn't believe in it. It was a concept which was distant from our sense of identity — we had no idea what it meant to be equal, and couldn't believe that it was possible.

* * *

What if someone had tried to say to Tsar Ivan the Terrible that everyone was equal before the law? I can imagine Ivan Vasilevich's reaction! Not just because he really was 'terrible', but because he was the sovereign anointed by God. How could other people be equal with him? Were they also anointed sovereigns? The Tsar answered only to God, therefore he was above any human court, which means he couldn't be equal to others. And if just one element of this system falls away, then the whole thing will stop working. If the will of one person is more important than the law, then the law is no longer required. Which means we can punish or pardon at will. Either the Tsar could, according to tradition, grant you the fur coat from his shoulders, or give the command and your head would roll from your shoulders. Often there was no reason behind to it. Often it was impossible to understand how and why it happened. But everyone realized that the most important thing was to be in favor with the ruler. And they would struggle endlessly to win that favor.

There are different names for it. Access to someone's ear, proximity, friends, circle of acquaintances, old school chums. Whatever you want to call it. The essence is the same — you want to be in favor with the ruler, to be on the inside. And with this state of affairs one and the same crime can lead either to a beating with the rod and torture on the rack, or to an embrace and a kiss of the Tsar's sweet lips. Just as the Emperor Peter the Great said to Aleksandr Danilovich Menshikov: 'Oh my dear Aleksey, oh you son of a bitch!' Have no doubts about it, that is how it still works. So heads will continue to roll and people will continue to steal. We can be sure of that. Because whether you live by the law or not, it does not mean you get to keep your head on your shoulders. Love and affection decide everything. What happens if his highness the emperor, the party first secretary, the president, or the minister don't like you? Then it's over for you! You might be the cleverest guy around, but you will have zero chance of getting ahead. And anyway, getting ahead could be the least of your worries.

Can you imagine someone in Tsarist Russia taking the Tsar to court? Or someone in the Soviet Union taking the general secretary of the Communist Party Central Committee to court? Or someone taking the President of the Russian Federation to court? It would be out of the question. Of course some smart ass will tell me now that you can't take the serving President of the US to court. That is you can't if he is still serving. But as soon as his term of office finishes, the criminal action can commence. But in Russia no one has even tried. The idea itself is strange. That's why until recently in Russia no former leader retired. They ruled until their deaths. They knew that to do otherwise would mean facing the hostility of the people they had ruled. They took pity on Khrushchev, but Gorbachev was tormented and put through terrible humiliations. And probably the only thing which prevented legal proceedings against Gorbachev was the close attention of the West. Otherwise it's not clear whether Mikhail Sergeevich could have ended up going the way of Yuliya Timoshenko. Knowing the feelings which Boris Nikolaevich harbored for Mikhail Sergeevich, such an outcome was quite possible. And you can be sure that they would have found a perfect legal basis for it. And no one would have doubted that it was nevertheless nothing to do with the law. Because the law in Russia is just pretty words for the Western media. But everyone knows how it really is. All that is important is who is in favor with the ruler.

Take for example the court case between Abramovich and Berezovsky taking place in London. This is a judgment day for Russia because it reveals how much of what happened in the 1990s was not legitimate, in particular the way in which the so called oligarchs acquired their property. The laws were made to be particularly favorable to these robbers, but they even managed to break these. And what about it? Does this mean that we can take them to court in Russia? Of course not. Don't tell me that you can just call the judge to get the right verdict. Or that you can bribe him. Because the more we continue to repeat this pattern of behavior, the clearer it becomes that the country can never develop in a civilized way.

What sort of country is it, after all, where the judges, who should treat everyone as equal, are themselves corrupt. Where Themis, she whose eyes must be bound, looks in the direction she is told to. What has happened to the declared aim of equality of all before the law? This is no country, but the mother of all corruption. Equality can only be achieved by legal means. The court must uphold the equality of all before the law. But does Russia even have a legal culture? The answer is unfortunately no. There have been attempts, there is plenty of experience — only that this is the experience of Communist summary justice. And what about our judges, who were said to take decisions on the basis of the law and 'gut instinct'. Pure genius — what on earth was this 'gut instinct'? Maybe it came from their sympathy for the aims of the Party, or the hints from their immediate superiors?

* * *

It has recently become popular to refer to the case of Sergey Magnitsky as an example of the horrors of our court system. My views on that specific case are not clear cut, but we're not dealing with that now. Let's be clear: the death of anyone in their cell awaiting trial is horrific. Anyone at all. Whether Magnitsky, not Magnitsky, some unfortunate woman who has been accused of swindling — it should not happen by principle. People are raped and killed in our pre-trial detention cells. It's a systemic problem. The criminals who allowed Magnitsky to die should be punished regardless of whether he himself was guilty or not.

When we say that our police force is no good, no one can argue with that. When we say that scoundrels, thieves and criminals are entrenched in our law enforcement agencies, and that they themselves should be in prison, no one can argue with that either. In Russia people get promoted for committing all manner of atrocities — and that's not the end of it, generally the more stars on their epaulettes, the more repulsive it is to have to look at their mugs. We can't argue with that.

But despite all of this, the problem in fact lies elsewhere. It is a complex and confused problem. No one should die in a pre-trial detention system. I repeat: no one should die in prison. No one. So when the human rights activists shout about Khodorkovsky and Magnitsky, refusing to see the horrors happening every day, every minute, every second to ordinary people who are arrested in their masses, I ask whether they are real human rights activists or biased scum. But I never get an answer. I have always thought that in the first place we should help those who can't even afford a solicitor. But in Russia we help those people who can afford to buy off anyone they want. That's the real problem.

And this means that what we need in the country are entirely new courts and new judges, who will forgot about socialist expedience, about loyalty to the Party, about phone calls from their friends, about class hatred, and will base their decisions entirely on the letter of the law — I don't dare to talk about the spirit of the law, because that often turns out to be tainted in Russia. This means that the court system needs to be entirely reformed. The judicial branch of power is one of the most important, because everything happening today will sooner or later impact on our common future, because the next generation will grow up and will treat lawlessness as lawful. And there is nothing we will be able to say to argue against it — in fact, look at all the executions and repressions during Comrade Stalin's times, which were all committed in line with the law. Did that make the law any better? Better to say that it made the law no less awful.

That is probably why this strange disjuncture between fairness and legality came about in Russia. Our country is probably the only one in the world where these terms don't have a similar meaning. Instead they have almost opposite meanings. Because when a Russian wants fairness it does not normally mean the legal process and a court ruling. The fairness we want to see is often strange and bloody. But what can we do — that is our history, our national character, our country. We are ruled by emotions. Everything has to be all or nothing, we don't like these long, complicated, clever and subtle processes. Instead we want everything to happen immediately and be readily comprehensible. The English might be happy to sit with their long legal processes and determine who, what, how, where to put the commas. It's completely different here in Russia. Our oligarchs sitting in that English court don't have a clue what is going on. Although, it should also be said that the English lawyers don't understand what our guys are talking about. It's a collision of two entirely different mentalities. One mentality, our mentality, is kind of mediaeval, the other is a Western one, no better and no worse, but completely different.

CHAPTER 13

From our school days we have been convinced that if we did badly in our exams and got a low mark, then that meant that not only did we know the subject badly, but that we were a bad person as well. We are probably the only country in the world where it is assumed that a star pupil is a better person than the pupil who gets worse marks. But there is absolutely no reason for drawing that conclusion. The start pupil might know the subject matter better, but that certainly doesn't mean that he has better personal qualities. Although for some reason we really believe that to be the case. And if someone is a better person then he is allowed to get away with more. So it's possible to see certain elements of corruption at play as early as school: the teachers have their pets, who really are allowed to get away with more than the others. Maybe somewhere far away, in some English private schools, it is customary to punish the pupils even if they are guilty of nothing, so that they don't get the idea that everything in life is going to be easy. In our schools the life of a teacher's pet is quite different from the lives of those pupils whom the teacher doesn't like for some reason.

This system is perpetuated throughout our entire lives. If a person becomes a middle manager then he is already a better person than those whom he issues his commands to. And the higher he climbs, the more he genuinely believes that he becomes even better, not just as a professional but as a person. For some reason, in Russia any minor job title gives a person the right to begin broadcasting his views. For some reason he begins to talk to you with a superior tone, to tell you what to do, and to behave provocatively stupidly. For some reason he naively assumes that if he has been appointed as boss, then he has automatically been awarded all the diplomas of all the institutes and academies in existence and has acquired the wisdom of the world. And if, heaven forbid, he has become the top boss, then watch out! As a minimum he will behave like comrade Stalin, who thought that he knew something about linguistics. He is happy to discuss any subject, but he can't entertain the thought that he might be wrong. What do you mean I'm wrong? With my job title how can I be wrong? But even the Tsars, the sovereigns anointed by God, could be wrong. Unfortunately no single person in the world has a monopoly on the truth.

Sometimes you hear how our statesmen, once in power, try to say profound things, and it is embarrassing to listen to. How can you tell them that wisdom doesn't come with the job? I always recall that wonderful joke told by Grigory Alekseevich Yavlinsky about Garri Kimovich Kasparov: 'Kasparov thinks that he is the champion of the world, but he forgets that he is only the champion of the world in chess.' Socrates, by contrast, did not hold a position in any ministry, and he is still considered a great wise man to this day.

* * *

We tend to assume, naively, that corruption is by definition possible only in the organs of power, that it is impossible to corrupt commercial structures, because that contradicts their very essence. But there are always opportunities for 'feeding'. It's clear after all that Telman Ismailov was appointed from above to the job he has. And it's clear that Deripaska was also. It's clear that the order has been given not to touch Prokhorov, so he is allowed to get away with a lot. But all of them have been appointed into rent-seeking positions. Although in recent times a major shift in the public consciousness has taken place, and everyone without exception feels it. The government has now begun to believe that it represents a higher form of truth.

In the 1990s we looked at the politicians and thought that these guys don't understand anything about business, let's sit down with them, have a talk, and explain how it all works. At that point various clubs came into being, which tried to convince various political actors that the state basically works according to a complicated business model. And that if the principles of corporate administration were applied, then the state would function wonderfully. This idea didn't work, and there are many reasons for that. One was that a company's activities are aimed at generating a profit, whereas in theory a state has different aims — although only in theory, especially when it comes to Russia.

So, we spoke with the politicians, explained the psychology of inter-personal relations, talked about how important it was to move the country forwards, to create market conditions, and we assured them that the market would resolve many problems by itself. And it seemed to us that these young guys with fire in their eyes — like Boris Nemtsov, Irina Khakamada, Yegor Gaidar, Chubais — would understand and would really create the conditions in which business could flourish.

Then came that first crisis, the most scary one, familiar from the history of how democracies normally develop, when the reformers begin to take the first steps. But then they stood still, because those first steps allowed them to gain a position of advantage, to divide up the resources into their own pockets and among their friends, and create their own elite, and they didn't want to let anyone else have a share of the pie. But they should have continued the forward momentum, because there is typically always a recoil phase in this kind of political development. In other words, in the 1996 elections Zyuganov should theoretically have won, so that the democrats could win again in 2000, but the democrats bought themselves victory in 1996, destroying the new democratic freedoms, preserving the system in the form it was in, and entering the period first of oligarchical capitalism, and then of bureaucratic feudalism, when capitalism stopped playing any role. This was when the institution of private property disappeared, just completely ceased to exist, and became just an object of ridicule, because no one strove to protect it, and the courts just did what they were told.

The most frightening thing is that the people in power still thought that there were some kinds of secret mechanisms which business understood better than them. How to compete in the global economy, how to negotiate with our Western partners, how the financial markets work. But then all of a sudden the international financial crisis happened. And the government could turn to the businessmen and say: 'So what now smart guys? What are you so down about? So you're all in debt? Asses left bare? Just come over here! How big are your debts?' Even a sad looking Deripaska turned up and was told: 'So you need money as well? But we know you won't give it back, you toad.' And of course he won't give it back, everyone knows that. But never mind that, he's a smart guy.

And so a remarkable situation came about, when the government suddenly understood that in fact it was the smart one. After all, the government could decide whom to give money to, and how much, which companies would live, which would get state support, whose billion rubles debts to the state would be written off, who would be allowed to breathe freely, and who could take part in the government spending program. Private companies could no longer decide anything at all. I spoke with a friend who moved across from business to the management of a very large bank. She told me that this was not banking as we know it. She was told who gets what, at what interest rate, and for what term. And she just saluted and answered 'Yes, sir.' The government has realized that businessmen are actually nobodies. Every single one of them. And so it has completely stopped listening to them.

Look at how bureaucrats now talk to people. They are like gods. There is nothing they can't do. Whether Monaco or London, they'll fix any problem, they know everyone there, they'll phone their man, have a word. Olympics, football? They're the ones to talk to. They decide who gets what, they'll fix it so everything will be just fine. What about the newspapers? So some English guys found some corruption going on? Oh dear me. You made it worse for yourselves, lost in the first round. Just don't try fighting the system. Bureaucrats of the world unite!

* * *

You know what amazes me about all of this? That the Russian people, who have adored the fairy story *The Naked King* from childhood, don't follow its lesson in real life. Not ever. Although they can still be in raptures over all manner of silly things, watching adoringly, hanging on every word. In the Soviet period there was a joke about the economy. If you worked in the social sciences then naturally you could not avoid Lenin's inheritance. Which meant that you would study, in particular, his book *On the so-called question of markets*. That book elaborates on the law established by Marx, which states that the manufacture of the means of production grows faster than the production of the means of consumption. But it is actually impossible to establish such a law. Because the forefathers of Marxism-Leninism made some sort of arithmetical mistake in the tables. But then that is not important, because the great leader never makes mistakes. Based on what the anecdote says — it may not be true, but it reflects our present-day mentality well — people learned the text with the mistake included, just in case. It was simpler like that. Heaven forbid you disprove the laws of the founding fathers, whatever would happen next? You wouldn't succeed in proving anything to anyone, you would just end up being branded an enemy of the people for the rest of your life. Better just to quietly learn the text with the arithmetical mistake included.

Maybe everyone understood that the idea of building Communism in a single country was complete nonsense, but since no one felt like arguing, they agreed: sure, by 1980 Communism will have arrived in Russia. Well, we did get the Olympics, that's not too bad. I wonder how many of those who promised Communism lived until 1980? As they say, you might promise to get married, but that doesn't mean you will. In Russia that phrase explains a lot. To talk of the equality of all before the law does not mean you have to implement it. Not one bit. And anyway, what fool thought up that idea in the first place? Does it really mean that everyone is equal? So if a great musician turns out to be a pedophile, does he have to answer for that just like everyone else? It's an uncomfortable question. Better to make something up instead. Pay someone some money, so it turns out that he wasn't a pedophile at all, he just taught young boys to play the piano, only his methods were a bit unusual. Before you know it, everyone has forgotten. And we will declare anyone who said a single bad word about him enemies of art, scoundrels, and awful prejudiced people. So is it really possible to imagine that everyone could be equal before the law!

So the more we talk about corruption in Russia, the more we realize that we can't irradicate it just like that. That is why I always say that the main problem with the phrase 'corruption in Russia' is not the word corruption, but the word Russia. For us corruption is just a way of life. Not just a means of redistributing financial resources, but a system by which we build our relations with each other. We really believe that it is the fair way of doing things. That this is just how it should be. That people can't be equal before the law. If I am the boss — you are shit, and vice versa. So if you are the boss you can humiliate your staff, shout at them, insult them. In Russia it's normal for the boss to use the Russian familiar form of 'you'. And as his junior you have to treat him with respect, using the polite form. It means nothing that he might be three times younger than you. He's the boss! So he's important! A real VIP!

If we think about it, it's clear that there has never been any real fight against corruption in Russia. For thousands of years, no less, the powers that be have simply fought to redistribute resources under the banner of fighting corruption — and that is how it will continue. It may be possible to combat the embezzlement of state funds, and even to keep it within some reasonable limits. But that is probably all you can do. Corruption will still exist. Some tasty morsel will always be found. If it's not embezzlement, then the handing out of food rations at the factory. If not that, then the holiday packages. If not that, then office space. Where no regulations exist, then arbitrary rule begins, and sycophancy follows swiftly. And every bureaucrat begins to think that he really is entitled to the public's respect.

It's funny, but it seems like everyone in Russia knows full well that at any moment you could either leap ahead of the game, or fall out completely. Just take a look — around the world the title of ambassador is given to those honorable people while they are still in office, but it also gives a title for life: whatever you do afterwards you will remain His Excellency Mr Ambassador for your whole life. But in Russia? So you're an ambassador. So does that mean you did your job badly, and they sent you off somewhere abroad? So you're a career diplomat and you don't know how to do anything else? It happens, you poor thing. And if you then lose the job of ambassador, why do you get to keep the title? Is it supposed to be some great honor to meet you? In fact we haven't had any real titles in Russia for almost one hundred years. There just isn't any sense in them at all.

Maybe in the past if you were his Highness the prince, then whatever position you served in you would still be a prince. Even if you were dismissed, you would still be a prince. And you lived like a prince, and people treated you differently, so you really felt you were a prince. But these days, you might think that you are a minister or member of the Central Committee, but tomorrow it turns out that you are an enemy of the people. And you wife is no princess, and no minister's spouse, but the wife of an enemy of the people. And you won't be going to your estate, to organize theatre for the serfs, but to the socialist building site to fell trees. And there you will tell everyone how you used to be a minister of fine breeding. But now you are no one. Because they took you from the shit, and made a candy out of you, but you can easily end up in the shit again. So you know that your time is limited and that tomorrow everything might end. The clock will chime, and the carriage will turn into a pumpkin, and the coachman into a mole, and you really don't want that! You don't want to see how the horses turn into mice, and your former friends and colleagues into your tormenters and betrayers. So while you are still here, you steal as much as you possibly can, and corrupt everyone around you at the same time. You lean on the people under you, but pay your dues to your bosses. You make your contacts left right and center, and just like a spider you weave your web, so that if, heaven forbid, something should happen, you get your early alarm signal and your can disappear quickly.

* * *

At one point the Communists got carried away with a strange idea, borrowed from the students of Freud. The idea was formulated by Marx and Engels, and then further developed by Lenin. The essence was the creation of a new form of person, *homo soveticus*. They thought that it would be possible to entirely remake the human character, creating an entirely new type of person, the builder of socialism. But the experiment didn't work — unfortunately no one had changed human genetics. And equally unfortunately our national character came into play. All attempts to transfer western experience to Russian soil — whether the fight against corruption or new legislation — have never produced any results. I won't discuss the Viking period, which is the stuff of legends, but if we look at the historical accounts then it's clear that whenever foreigners came here, even in the most favorable of circumstances, starting with the time of Peter I, they ended up having the same experience as the conquerors of ancient China: they arrived with their foreign languages but still ended up speaking Chinese and adopting the great Chinese culture for themselves.

Just the same in Russia. People might have tried to set Russia on a different path, their intentions may have been noble, great philosophers may have corresponded with our Majesties the Emperors and Empresses, but in the end the Russian spirit — or call it corruption — always won out. What's more, yesterday's Harvard boys, German barons, and decorated French thinkers just took as much as they could from Russia. They just couldn't stop. And they behaved in a way that we Russians could never dream of behaving. Whether in the 18th century, the end of the 20th century, or the 21st century. They came here, and it was as if they had forgotten all their Protestant or Catholic principles, they behaved in a way we locals — savages as they saw us — could never dream of behaving. After some time passed some of them were taken to court — as in the case of the American privatizers — but they still shake their heads in amazement: what horrors these unfortunate pioneers had to encounter in the wind-swept wilds of Russia! And what was there to take from these Russian barbarians anyway? It's just a wild, lawless, country. And so one of the most ancient peoples in the world, with one of the most ancient histories finds itself again and again in the role of some sort of wild man, whom others don't respect, but only fear — especially when he has his nuclear cudgel.

The apathy which stifles us also has a reverse side — the riot. After all it is much easier, instead of enduring exhausting legal battles, to send the whole thing to damnation, take a rock, and smash in the judge's head. A different kind of justice. It's easier than going from office to office, spreading slander, trying to prove your case. You don't need to prove anything. That's how it has always been in Russia. Even our great Russian literature does not give a single clear example in support of the belief that all should be equal before the law. Nothing of the sort. We don't even have the genre of court novel. We've got the crime genre, detective novels. But what about the court novel, where the judge is the center of attention? Try to think of just one classic of Russian literature where the court process was the center of the story or the main hero was a judge. Or even a secondary character who appeared for one episode. Or something about how the unfortunate hero ends up in front of a wise judge who changes his whole life by passing a just verdict. Remember that one?

You will have to think long and hard trying to remember, and I'm more than certain that nothing will come to mind. Possibly the only thing you might think of is the genre of criminals songs, when the unlucky bandit is being tried, and it turns out that he is in fact the son of the prosecutor, and of course he faces the firing squad. That's probably the only example. In other words, there is not a single positive example of a judge in Russian literature and art. And no one trusts the courts. That is almost totally absent in our culture. No wise parables of Solomon, no attempts to decide who is right and who is wrong. Instead popular culture represents the deeply ingrained conviction that not only are we not equal before the law, but that no one needs the law anyway, since everything is decided by personal contacts. And you are told that you will never experience justice in your life, maybe only after your death, but that the higher you manage to climb the ladder, the less chance that you will have a heavy fall. The system of personal contacts will not let you down. And this system looks after its own, so there is no equality before the law, and there can never be.

So corruption in Russia is multi-layered and complex, it resembles a cancerous tumor, which spreads by metastasis. You can see this in the inequality of society, in the embezzlement of public funds, in the ineffective police and justice systems. But where do the roots of this lie? Where did it all start? Not from the imperfections of our laws, or the absence of the necessary administrative procedures. But rather from the fact that within ourselves we feel no real need for it to be any different. We might get really upset if we don't get our share of the pie. But if we are lucky enough to get even a large crumb for ourselves, how easily we are able to bypass the law, even if earlier we thought it sacred and we criticized anyone who tried to break it.

Give an honest answer: if tomorrow you were offered one of those flashing VIP lights for your car, and there would be no negative consequences of taking it, would you be able to turn it down? Or let's say just an ID card you could wave at the police when they stop you, so that everything would be OK. In fact, even those flashing lights are a form of corruption. They are a means of showing that one person is more important than the other. We've got the traffic regulations, not quite law, but almost. But then we've got those people who are equal, and then those who are a bit more equal. I've been proposing for some time now that we take the system to its logical conclusion. Judge for yourself: you're driving down the road, you've got your flashing light, everyone sees and knows that it is you. But then what happens when you get out of the car? I suggest making small lights the same size as a deputy's badge. Or if you need, heaven forbid, to visit the shopping center, you can have a hat with a flashing light. So that everyone makes way for you as you go to the cash desk. It's nice for you, and convenient for everyone else, since they all know who is coming. But then again, since so many flashing lights have now appeared, you need to introduce some way of distinguishing between the people using them. After all, it's just no good if everyone is the same.

* * *

In his day the great Roman Emperor Trajan formulated the ideal maxim for all rulers. He said that he would like to be the kind of ruler for his people that he would like to see as ruler if he were one of the people. Looking at our history, can we say that any of our rulers have abided by this rule? No, unfortunately it has never happened.

We have forgotten two great names. If I could I would force everyone who wants to become a state official to read the history of Ancient Rome. Not Ancient Greece — the Greeks had no idea about state building, they came up with some entirely worthless and unusable ideas about administration, flooded the world with empty terms, and no one knows what to do with them now. We must study the history of Ancient Rome. Not just in the fourth or fifth grade at school, but in detail at institute level. Regardless of what profession they go into, everyone should be obliged to know two great names, and a particular famous Roman saying should become entirely familiar to everyone. To be precise, it is a wish, which sounds as follows: 'so as to be happier than Augustus and better than Trajan'.

Augustus and Trajan. Two great men, founders of empires, who laid the foundations of modern statehood as it exists to this day. We must take this wisdom into account, it is extremely important to do so.

What did Augustus, who was incidentally terribly unhappy in his personal life, say? He was the first of the emperors to begin to tackle his people's sins, insisting that having children was compulsory, that anyone who did not would be fined, anyone who was unmarried would also be fined, and that anyone guilty of debauchery would be punished.

When he issued the law punishing people for debauchery, the emperor gave concessions to no one. His own daughter was unfaithful to her husband under the gaze of all of Rome, so Augustus sent her into exile. Incidentally, this was why Ovid, who wrote all that foolish verse poetry, got his comeuppance as a corrupter of morals. He felt the full wrath of Augustus who was suffering the loss of his daughter and wife, after they had both gone off into exile together. Ovid was also sent into exile and died on the territory of modern day Moldova. Moldova and Crimea were the Roman versions of Siberia — Moldova for the decent guys, and Crimea for the Jews.

Augustus was the first person to correctly formulate how a ruler should manage relations with the provinces. He said that a wise ruler would act as a shepherd, who sheers the wool from the sheep, but does not kill them.

Trajan was the emperor under whom the Roman army reached the height of its powers. Under him — two thousand years ago — the first field hospital in history appeared, because the legion would not begin its march without its own doctors, and a retired legionary would get a plot of land, a luxurious house and money, so military service was considered a privilege. He was the first emperor to be born outside the borders of Rome, on the territory of modern day Spain.

Oh, and he loved to drink. If Boris Nikolaevich Yeltsin had studies history, he would have followed Trajan's example. What did it involve? Trajan told his people not to implement the orders which he gave after a long banquet. But if Yeltsin had been forced to study the history of Ancient Rome, we would still to this day be living in the Soviet Union, because all the leaders who signed the agreement in the Belovezhskaya forest had, to put it politely, had a little tipple to calm their nerves — so no one would have implemented their orders!

Trajan's personal guard was very important to him, he gave a dagger to the man in charge and told him to defend him with this weapon if he was right, but to turn it against him if he was not. Which of our leaders could have said something like that? And who would have lived more than two weeks if they had said it? It's a tough question. Think about it, could Yeltsin have said those words, handing a dagger to his personal guard? What about the leaders of our republics in the North Caucasus? And what about all those regional leaders who have long lost all sense of shame and are stealing left right and center?

The system of 'feeding' would not exist in Russia if we had an educated, enlightened ruler. Such a ruler could be trained, but that would not be enough. The main thing which could counter the system of 'feeding' is the institution of private property. Why is it that not a single one of us would refrain from using illegal means, in one way or another, to ensure a decent living standard for our family? It is because there is no private property in Russia. There is only talk about it, declarations. But it is all just lies.

Take a look, is anyone in Russia living in a home left to them by their forefathers? Does anyone have any possessions at all which were left by their forefathers — apart from maybe a pair of silver teaspoons, a fifty kopeck piece, and a little china cut with a chipped rim. Maybe two books written with the old Russian alphabet. And that's it. Where is the house, where is the garden with hundred-year-old apple trees, where is granny's chest, stuffed full of treasures? Instead, everyone had to start from scratch, by thieving. Every time someone starts a new job, he starts with his ass bare and a load of children to feed. And so he thieves as much as he can, hoping that when his good fortune ends, and everything he has acquired is shaken from him, then maybe a crumb will remain lodged between his fingers, and his kids will at least be able to scrape something together to live off. Because even the all-powerful Menshikov finished his days a pauper.

* * *

Someone made a very accurate observation in response to one of my blogs. He wrote that slavery did not end after the civil war in America. In reality, it ended when the black girl refused to stay in the part of the bus allocated to black people. In 1861 serfdom was repealed in Russia. But did we cease to be serfs? Let's take an honest look at ourselves.

We live in a country where all our ideas about life have been turned on their head. There is an old story about how Leonid Parfenov is appearing somewhere and says that he is very worried that there are no longer any real news programs in Russia — although he doesn't say who or what exactly he means. So everyone is in raptures — what a brave thing to say! But he didn't say this in front of a TV camera. He said it during an internet broadcast, and he didn't name a single guilty party, didn't give a single concrete example, and didn't say anything about how the system really works. But in response everyone agreed with him, called for us to be free to watch real news, and described Parfenov as a hero!

Forgive me, but what prevented Parfenov from showing real news on his program on Channel One? What prevented him going up to each of the newsreaders and telling them that he didn't see the corpses of murdered newscasters and editors littering the streets of Hero city Moscow. He didn't see processions of convicts leaving the TV studios. He didn't ask them what they were afraid of. Or if they were trying to keep hold of their jobs. Or ask who could be sacked, if everyone spoke the truth. What could anyone do to them? If they thought that they had been unfairly dismissed, they could go to court, and defend themselves! But no, this was instead the whine of a serf to his lord: 'Lord, please let me be free!' It was just servile behavior.

Before that one 'Yura Shevchuk, musician' asked Putin a question on one of his phone-ins. But who did you think you were talking to Yura? Putin is just a servant of the people. He works for the salary which we pay him. And you are a citizen. So why do you speak with him like he is a Tsar and you are a serf? Maybe it's because you are an idiot, Yura. Everyone said that he was so brave, that he spoke the truth right to Putin's face. But he didn't even take an active position as a citizen. The prime minister can't do what is beyond his powers.

In 1861 we repealed serfdom, but we still didn't become free. We still have this mentality which tells us that certain things are forbidden. We are waiting for the permission to be free. No one takes personal responsibility. They say that every village in Russia is like Kushchevka. But what exactly was Kushchevka? Kushchevka showed only one thing: that we are slaves, miserable, insignificant slaves. How many of those bandits were there? Two hundred? The population of Kushchevka is thirty thousand. There were Cossacks amongst them, and former soldiers. There may even be some real men amongst them. Those bandits murdered and raped for fifteen years — there were two hundred women raped there, and that is only those who reported it. Imagine — they get home, somebody's wife, sister or daughter, they tell their husbands, fathers or brothers what happened, and in reply they get 'Just put up with it, at least you weren't killed'. Is that really normal?

They didn't go to get revenge, they even didn't take their wives out of that hell, they just carried on living there. Strong, healthy men stroke their wives on the heads and tell them they've got no money, so they can't leave there, it's where they were born and where they will stay. They didn't even move to the neighboring village, they did nothing. They are just like cattle, so that's why they got slaughtered. When those twelve unlucky souls were killed, they say that the shrieking was so loud that the villagers' hair stood on end from horror. But according to the police statements, no one heard anything. That really is a terrible indictment of our people.

We constantly tell ourselves that when the Russian people rise up they show no remorse. Pure lies. If we tell it straight, then the sad truth is that we are serfs. And the lords still rule over us, not because they are worthy, but because we are so afraid of everything. Even when there is nothing to be afraid of. Serfdom was repealed, but we remained slaves. Just take a look at yourselves, you're perfectly presentable, and you're standing up straight! You're not some sort of prison trash! We recall the glory of the Warsaw ghetto uprising, when people knew that they were going to their death, but fought tooth and nail against the fascist scum. And then, in contrast, there is the shame of Babi Yar, when people stood in line for the firing squad, obediently waiting for their bullet. But we always have a choice, even when it seems that there is no other way.

Although after Kushchevka we had the Sagra case, when the cars carrying sixty bandits armed to their teeth were stopped by eight brave men with hunting rifles, accompanied by their women, who came with pitchforks and crow-bars to help.

But we are so used to giggling, laughing, having fun, putting on appearances that nothing is wrong, that in the end we just skim the surface of life, failing to realize that at some point we are going to have to bequeath something to our children. But what can we give them? That same slave's yoke, and our only piece of wisdom, carried through the generations, that you have to be quiet, not stick out too much, know how to make friends, and wait for your chance, when you get your cozy position where you can 'feed'. There is no corruption in Russia, only a herd of slaves, who are sometimes lucky enough to stand under a golden ray of sunlight and for a moment feel bathed in the sweetness of being.

Serfdom did not go anywhere. I don't know how many years have to pass before we fully understand the responsibility each of us bears, the need for everyone to respect the institution of private property, to care about others' opinions and others' wellbeing. We have given no one a dagger to be used against those in power, because that dagger is turned against all the Russian people, because every one of us is ready to put up with things as they are, hoping that when the chance comes his way, when that lucrative position is free, he will take it and trample his predecessor into the dirt.

* * *

On 4 December 2011 elections to the sixth State Duma took place in Russia. Straight after the count a large number of people expressed indignation at how the results had been falsified. Thousands took part in the demonstrations, and probably the largest of them took place in Moscow on Bolotnaya Square.

It's hard for me to say how far those who took part were in the right, and whether their accounts are honest. I can't pass judgment in place of the court. But for me a question arises: what happens next? *The New York Times* is already writing that Nemtsov is the leader and that he has gathered together between thirty and fifty thousand people — it's not important exactly how many. People are saying that they have come to support Nemtsov. But what will we remember of all this when some time has passed? How many of us remember who called together the protestors in 1991? We remember only that Yeltsin appeared on top of the tank, and the same will be true of these recent events.

Ask yourself: whose money has Nemtsov been living off? He didn't actually have any money of his own. Maybe that very same Mikhail Prokhorov helped him a little bit? What money does Kasyanov live off? Did you know that as a former prime minister the state still supports him — he has still got his dacha and personal guard. No one asks what money Volodya Ryzhkov lives off. How do these people earn themselves an income, pay for their daily bread? Has anyone ever asked these questions? How do Chirikova or Oreshkin know how many people really voted for one party or another in Moscow? Where do they get this information from? Or maybe they are gods of some sort? Did they just go and pray and get all that information just like that?

The main problem here is the eternal tolerance of the Russian people. I remember how in 1991, when real civil society started to appear, people went to the White House to die, because they went up against the tanks and the KGB, and Yeltsin went to the demonstration knowing that a sniper could easily kill him, or that he could be knocked off on the way there. You might laugh, but the greatest Russian martyrs, the trailblazers of civil society, were those six people who walked out on to Red Square to protest against our troops being sent to Czechoslovakia. They knew very well that they could be wiped out completely, that their lives could be destroyed, but they went all the same.

Those people who went out on to Bolotnaya Square were not really in any danger. There were no tanks, or long prison sentences threatening them. None of that. These people don't know what they are talking about when they declare that they have established civil society in Russia. The majority of them are from the generation that have not witnessed death in their lifetimes. They didn't experience the war in Chechnya, they didn't see blood on the streets of Moscow, they don't remember 1993 and the tanks firing on the White House. They don't remember any of that at all. But I do remember, it happened in my lifetime, in front of my eyes.

But we're not talking about that now. These people went out to protest, and had the right to do so. But whom, or what, where they supporting? What did they want to achieve? Did they want the elections to be honest? I'm in favor of that too. But who made these elections unfair? Will those scum answer for falsifying the results, stuffing the ballot boxes, tampering with the votes, and everything else they did? How many of those people were there? Why is no one saying that every single one of them should be punished?

I've got my personal point of view on this. It's very simple: the government has long since stopped listening to the people! But demonstrations are not enough to make the government listen, constant pressure is needed. I have always said that we need to fight corruption properly, not by simply redirecting the flows of money from the corrupt people of the 1990s to the corrupt people of the 2000s. I have always said that we have to put people in prison. We need to see dismissals among the leadership of the security ministries, we need Golikova and Fursenko to be dismissed. And I am still saying these things to this day. I am still saying that we need courts, courts which are free, honest and independent.

By the way, I have realized why oligarchs always go to court overseas. Because here in Russia their riches and everything else are hidden behind offshore companies, whereas over there they have to come into the open. So when the court case takes place overseas, they can demand real assets in payment if they win. It's interesting to see that all those people who spent the 1990s molding the Russian government to suit their purposes are now so frightened of falling into the clutches of the legal system which they created. They are happy to go to court anywhere, as long at it's not Russia.

I always call for concrete measures. Take for example that terrible tragedy, when the governor of Sverdlovsk region died in hospital after a traffic accident. Of course you and I know that it cost votes for the United Russia party. So I firmly believe that all these people should have the flashing lights on their cars taken away from them. Only the police and emergency services should have them, because no one else needs them. When the president or prime minister is travelling by car, the roads are anyway closed, so the flashing lights aren't needed. But when the Minister for the Economy Elvira Nabiulina holds up the whole of Tverskaya Street and makes a massive diversion with her flashing light, who is it good for? And would it really be so terrible if Minister Nabiulina is late for work, even if she is late by twenty seven years? Nabiulina is sweet, intelligent, kind — and completely inconsequential. Why does she need a flashing light?

What's more, I reckon that due to the public interest in the accidents which they get into, all state vehicles which transport VIPs should be equipped with video recording equipment and satellite tracking systems, which will then be able to establish their exact route. If this type of accident takes place, no one should be in any doubt about who is guilty and who is innocent, so that it doesn't end up like on Lenin Prospect. No doubts at all. And if for some reason it proves impossible to clearly establish what happened, or the video recording doesn't work, or something else happens, then the VIP would automatically be found guilty.

During the pre-election debate two arguments could be heard with great frequency. The first was the need for the ratification of the twentieth article of the Convention on Combatting Corruption, which introduces accountability not only for income but outgoings as well. Almost all parties supported this idea. And the second, after the court case in the UK which I have referred to, was that the public is no longer prepared to hear those fairy stories about how there was no choice but to transfer the country's wealth into private hands. People have had enough of the lies! Everyone knows that the country's wealth was robbed. And the thieves should be brought before a court of law and punished. Everything that was stolen should be transferred back into public ownership, and then we can decide what to do with it, how to divide it up.

I realize that a large number of candidates will pop up, asking that they be let close to the feeding trough, convinced that they will do a better job of managing the national wealth. That is why I think that all state enterprises should be turned into concessions, like uncle Lenin did. Because as it currently stands we have, for example, Gazprom, a national resource, telling us in its adverts that dreams can come true. I'm very happy for them! But look at how ineffectively the company is managed! Why does Gazprom have its own football teams and all that other stuff? Can anyone tell me? To this day some villages in Russia don't even have gas. And even in those places where there is a gas supply nearby, getting connected to it can cost vast sums of money. So why does Gazprom spend money in a kind of drunken delirium on things which have nothing to do with its core business. Do the old ladies in their villages who have no heating or gas supply really care if the Zenit football team is champion? They couldn't give a damn about Zenit. Of course if Gazprom wants to treat this as a charitable activity, then let them do so, and use their profit for it. But how are they going to work out how much their profit is? Are they going to hike up our gas prices? If so, it's a very strange national resource. Why does the only structure which in theory has this national status spend money like the country is its fiefdom. This is exactly what I have been talking about in this book. They've been appointed to feed from the country's resources.

AFTERWORD

Russia is infected with corruption from head to toe. But does this mean that Russia has no future? Of course it doesn't. As a simple example, try to imagine an organism that has no bacteria. No such organism exists, because microbes are essential to life. It is another matter when the bacteria population grows beyond a certain critical boundary — it means that the organism is seriously ill. But when these bacteria exist in small numbers it suits everyone. It's the same with corruption — as long as it doesn't start to flourish, everyone is happy to tolerate it. But when shameless greed knows no boundaries, a cure has to be found. How can we find one if the structures which are set up to combat corruption themselves always turn into centers of rent-seeking? This means that the fight against corruption is just an expensive indulgence, which we have to pay for — although we could say that it will pay for itself, given how very profitable it can be. What kind of new broom do we need to sweep away this system, if that is even possible?

I believe that it is definitely possible. Anything is possible. If we don't believe that, then there is no sense in living. Can we do it quickly and easily? No, we can't. Do we need fundamental changes in order to do it? Yes, it's clear that we do. We need to start talking again about the freedom of the press, about government transparency, and the independence of the judges from 'telephone law' and bribery. Of course we need to talk about how the judges are appointed, and who is appointed, we need to talk about the court process itself, about the prosecution and the defense, and the solicitors' rights. All of that is true, and we all know it. But this is just the hardware, so to speak. As far as the software is concerned, the soul, than we have to recognize that even if corruption is manifested in many different forms, its true nature is always the same, and it is part of our national character. We need to cure this infection, starting with clear, tough, concrete measures. By changing the court system. By changing the relationship between the government and society. By guaranteeing the equality of all before the law, beginning with ourselves, with our own wives, parents, children, friends, school-friends, colleagues — everyone. Everyone must be equal before the law, however frightening that thought may be at first.

And it's also essential that those people who occupy the highest government positions set a positive example to society. The essence of this can be summed up in that nasty formula which I won't refrain from repeating, and which not a single government in the world actually wants to implement: 'Beat your own people in order to scare the others, and do as I do.'

Or as the wise Confucius said: 'To govern is to improve oneself. Who would dare not to improve themselves, if you yourself do so?'

Glagoslav Publications Catalogue

- *The Time of Women* by Elena Chizhova
- *Sin* by Zakhar Prilepin
- *Hardly Ever Otherwise* by Maria Matios
- *The Lost Button* by Irene Rozdobudko
- *Khatyn* by Ales Adamovich
- *Christened with Crosses* by Eduard Kochergin
- *The Vital Needs of the Dead* by Igor Sakhnovsky
- *METRO 2033* (Dutch Edition) by Dmitry Glukhovsky
- *METRO 2034* (Dutch Edition) by Dmitry Glukhovsky
- *A Poet and Bin Laden* by Hamid Ismailov
- *Asystole* by Oleg Pavlov
- *Kobzar* by Taras Shevchenko
- *White Shanghai* by Elvira Baryakina
- *The Stone Bridge* by Alexander Terekhov
- *King Stakh's Wild Hunt* by Uladzimir Karatkevich
- *Depeche Mode* by Serhii Zhadan
- *Saraband Sarah's Band* by Larysa Denysenko
- *Herstories*, An Anthology of New Ukrainian Women Prose Writers
- *Watching The Russians* (Dutch Edition) by Maria Konyukova
- *The Hawks of Peace* by Dmitry Rogozin
- *The Grand Slam and Other Stories* (Dutch Edition) by Leonid Andreev
- *The Battle of the Sexes Russian Style* by Nadezhda Ptushkina
- *A Book Without Photographs* by Sergey Shargunov

More coming soon…

www.ingramcontent.com/pod-product-compliance
Lightning Source LLC
Chambersburg PA
CBHW032139020426
42334CB00016B/1217